The Family DISCIPLESHIP BIBLE

OLD TESTAMENT

CHRIS CHAVEZ

Illustrated by
MIKE BROWN

LUCIDBOOKS

The Family Discipleship Bible: Old Testament

Copyright © 2019 by Chris Chavez
Illustrations Copyright © 2019 by Mike Brown

Published by Lucid Books in Houston, TX
www.LucidBooksPublishing.com
and
Wyden Publishing in Katy, TX
www.wydenpublishing.com

All rights reserved. No part of this publication may be reproduced, stored in a retrieval system, or transmitted in any form by any means, electronic, mechanical, photocopy, recording, or otherwise, without the prior permission of the publisher, except as provided for by USA copyright law.

eISBN-10: 1-63296-353-1 | eISBN-13: 978-1-63296-353-6
ISBN-10: 1-63296-401-5 | ISBN-13: 978-1-63296-401-4

Unless otherwise indicated, all Scripture quotations are taken from the ESV® Bible (The Holy Bible, English Standard Version®), copyright © 2001 by Crossway, a publishing ministry of Good News Publishers. Used by permission. All rights reserved.

Scripture quotations marked (KJV) are taken from the King James Version (KJV): King James Version, public domain.

Special Sales: Most Lucid Books titles are available in special quantity discounts. Custom imprinting or excerpting can also be done to fit special needs. Contact Lucid Books at Info@LucidBooksPublishing.com.

To Heather Chavez—Thank you for who you are. I love you so much, but in putting this book together, I appreciate you in a way I never dreamed. As a helpmate, you are not just some helper who stands by your man, but you are absolutely necessary for me to do anything meaningful in the Kingdom. There is no Chavez family kingdom vision without you. I never knew what I needed, and even today I do not know how much of a blessing you will be to me in the years to come. You stand as the tangible evidence of God's great love for me on a daily basis. I love you and wish I could live out that love much better than I do. Hang in there because God will help me grow into the man you deserve.

To Antonio, Moriah, Samuel, and Thaddeus—This book was driven by my desire to give you as firm a foundation as possible. I can't change your heart, but I can teach you and point you to the good Father who loves you more than I ever will. One day, you will understand that I deeply desired to give you all that I never had. Daddy loves you!

To Dr. Freddie Gage (1933–2014)—Many people evangelize, but an evangelist is someone altogether different. Soul winning is what they breathe. Dr. Freddie Gage taught me more about evangelism just by being who God made him to be than any book or Bible lesson. Words cannot express how grateful I am to have known him. Beyond seeing the evangelistic gift at work, he showed me that loving people means doing what others won't do in order to love people.

Chris Chavez

I want to thank my father, Lt. Col. Gene E. Brown, who passed away during the production of this book. I also want to thank my mother, Regina Brown, whose strong will kept my father alive long enough to ensure his grandkids will always remember their "Pockets." To my loving wife, Cheree, and my four amazing children—Abby, Luke, Lydia, and Phoebe—God has graced me with the most loving family I certainly don't deserve. The patience they have shown me over these past two years, discussing the day's events while I was chained to my drawing table has been a true blessing. Last, I would also like to thank Kristin Bergh. Working with you on the colors is always a joy, and I know the difficulty you had working through the loss of your sister.

Michael Brown

Table of Contents

Getting Started with Family Discipleship
Welcome   2
Devotional Ideas and Templates   5
Tools Provided in This Book   10

Family Discipleship Bible Stories
Bible Stories   15

1. Before "in the Beginning"   17
2. The Creation of the World   21
3. The Creation of the Spirit World   25
4. The Fall of Man   29
5. The Story of Job   33
6. The Flood: Part 1   37
7. The Flood: Part 2   41
8. Tower of Babel: God Knows Everything   45
9. Abraham and Isaac: God Is Faithful   49
10. Ishmael's Story   53
11. Isaac and the Promise   57
12. Joseph: Part 1   61
13. Joseph: Part 2   65
14. Moses: Part 1   69
15. Moses: Part 2   73
16. Passover   77
17. Deliverance from Egypt   81
18. The Ten Commandments   85
19. God's Desire to Dwell with Man (the Tabernacle)   89
20. Joshua and the Spies   93

21	Jericho: Part 1	97
22	Jericho: Part 2	101
23	Samson	105
24	David Anointed King	109
25	David and Goliath	113
26	Solomon Builds God's Temple	117
27	Ecclesiastes: The Futility of Life	121
28	The Division of the Kingdom	125
29	Elijah on Mount Carmel	129
30	Jonah	133
31	Exile of Israel and Judah	137
32	Daniel and the Lions' Den	141
33	Hananiah, Mishael, and Azariah	145
34	Prophecy of the Coming King (Book of Isaiah)	149

Family Discipleship Bible Sound Off (Catechism)

Introductory (Ages 2–8)	154
Intermediate (Ages 6–12)	159
Jewish Bible Timeline (Ages 2+)	174

Family Discipleship Tools

Scripture Blessings	186
Family Dictionary	204
Songs for the Family	207
Summary of Old Testament Books	208
Scripture Memory Passages	213

In Conclusion

Final Message to Parents	222
Additional Resources for Your Home	226
Acknowledgments	230

Getting Started with Family Discipleship

Welcome, Parents!

We are so glad you've chosen to use this Bible. *The Family Discipleship Bible* was created to equip you as you follow God's command to teach your children the ways of the Lord. In Deuteronomy 6:4–7, we find the clearest call for parents to be the primary teachers in their children's lives.

> Hear, O Israel: The LORD our God, the LORD is one. You shall love the LORD your God with all your heart and with all your soul and with all your might. And these words that I command you today shall be on your heart. You shall teach them diligently to your children, and shall talk of them when you sit in your house, and when you walk by the way, and when you lie down, and when you rise.

Routine devotionals, whether daily or weekly, are only one aspect of discipleship. As you know, children are learning even when we are not intentionally teaching a specific lesson. So parents living out their beliefs are just as important as what they teach, and in most cases, it can be the biggest evangel to children. We truly believe that to be better parents, we must be transformed into the image of Christ more and more.

In the meantime, we hope this resource will help you plant seeds, water, and cultivate the soil of your children's hearts in the hope that God gives the increase (1 Cor. 3:6). Using this resource will strengthen your family relationships and

Welcome, Parents!

provide an opportunity for you to take the lead in being the primary teacher in your children's lives.

Remember, you are no longer under the law but under God's grace, so having regular devotionals does not earn you anything. That also means that not having regular devotionals does not make you less of a believer, and missing one or two does not bring you shame. There is no condemnation to those in Christ Jesus (Rom. 8:1), so please embark on this parenting journey as a free man who chooses to live as a slave to Christ.

Realize that the path to greater joy is found in fulfilling God's commands. Parents have the incredible opportunity to be part of God's story in the salvation of their children. God needs no one to bring about the salvation of a child, and no one can hinder God from saving a child either. But as we follow God's command of preaching the gospel and making disciples, we find our greatest joy.

Let us as parents embrace our built-in mission field: the home. There, we have the opportunity to freely proclaim the gospel daily in both word and deed. Once a child is saved, we have the built-in opportunity to disciple that child on a daily basis. This Bible is not *the* tool to help you, but it is *a* tool that we hope you find useful. Feel completely free to disagree with some theological concepts as you read the Bible stories and other texts.

Outside of the gospel, there is much freedom in the non-essentials, so if you do not like the wording in a particular story, by all means change it on the fly. The

same goes for the catechism. If you find another answer more true to scripture or more in line with what you hope to teach your children about God, please do so. This is not a Baptist, Catholic, Bible church, or Methodist devotional tool but rather a tool any parent can use who would like a little help pointing their child to the most high God. May you find joy in shepherding your family toward God in all things.

Blessings to your family,
Chris Chavez
Author

Devotional Ideas and Templates

What does a family devotional look like?

To be honest, what a family devotional looks like really depends on you. You can use these tools together or mix and match them as you see fit. For instance, if you feel your current devotionals are doing what you hoped they would do but want to start catechizing a bit, you might add a Bible Sound Off element. If that is the case, the catechisms will give you questions to ask your children daily, weekly, or even periodically. A great thing about catechizing is that in many cases, the parents learn the answers as well. So even new believers can disciple their children while they learn too.

The possibilities of what you can do together are endless. You can experiment and see what works best for your family. The good thing about devotionals is that they can evolve as your family grows in size and in the knowledge of God. This Bible is not intended to be a how-to manual but a resource for parents to maximize discipleship in the home.

What it will look like in your home is only limited by your imagination. We hope you sing, act out Bible stories, ask deep questions, and grow just as much as your children.

There are a few samples of how to creatively impart Bible stories on the next page.

Full Devotionals

1. **Toddler Age: Daily or Weekly Devotional before Bed (20–30 minutes)**
   - ♣ Read Bible Story (5–10 minutes)
     - ♦ The Jesus Storybook Bible is excellent for toddlers
     - ♦ Ask simple questions and dialogue about the story
   - ♣ Bible Sound Off (5 minutes)
   - ♣ Sing Together (5 minutes)
   - ♣ Listen (1 minute)
   - ♣ Family Prayer (5 minutes)
     - ♦ Family, friends, the lost, government leaders
   - ♣ Scripture Blessing (2 minutes)

2. **Elementary Age: Daily or Weekly Devotional before Bed (25–40 minutes)**
   - ♣ Read Bible Story (5–10 minutes)
     - ♦ Ask questions and dialogue about the story
   - ♣ Bible Sound Off (5 minutes)
   - ♣ Scripture Memorization (5 minutes)
   - ♣ Sing Together (5–10 minutes)
   - ♣ Family Prayer (5–10 minutes)
     - ♦ Family, friends, the lost, government leaders
     - ♦ Listen occasionally*
   - ♣ Scripture Blessing (2 minutes)

Devotional Ideas and Templates

3. **Mixed Ages: Daily or Weekly Devotional before Bed (30–45 minutes)**
   - Read Bible Story (10–15 minutes)
     - Act out a story
   - Bible Sound Off (10 minutes)
   - Scripture Memorization (5 minutes)
   - Family Prayer (5–10 minutes)
     - Family, friends, the lost, government leaders
   - Scripture Blessing (2 minutes)
   - Parent sings song over each child as final good night
     - Rock smaller children when possible

4. **Mixed Ages: Daily or Weekly Devotional before Bed (25–40 minutes)**
   - Read Bible Story (10–15 minutes)
     - Answer questions and dialogue about the story
     - Let them lead the dialogue
   - Sing Together (10–15 minutes)
   - Family Prayer (5–10 minutes)
     - Family, friends, the lost, government leaders
     - Listen occasionally*
   - Scripture Blessing (2 minutes)

Partial Devotionals (Late Nights, Driving Home, Hectic Day)

1. **Toddler Age: (10–15 minutes)**
   - Parents Read Story from Jesus Story Book Bible (5 minutes)
     - Highlight important themes, ideas

- Family Prayer (5 minutes)
    - Family, friends, the lost, government leaders
- Father's Blessing (2 minutes)

2. Mixed Ages: (10–15 minutes)

- Parents Read Bible Story from Any Children's Bible
    - Highlight important themes, ideas
- Family Prayer (5 minutes)
    - Family, friends, the lost, government leaders
- Father's Blessing (2 minutes)

3. Mixed Ages: (10–15 minutes)

- Bible Sound Off (5 minutes)
- Family Prayer (5 minutes)
    - Family, friends, the lost, government leaders
- Father's Blessing (2 minutes)

4. Mixed Ages: (15–25 minutes)

- Read Bible Story (5–10 minutes)
    - Highlight key ideas
- Family Prayer (5–10 minutes)
    - Family, friends, the lost, government leaders
- Father's Blessings (2 minutes)

Other Simple Devotional Ideas

1. Act out a Bible story with homemade costumes.
2. Teach children your favorite worship songs.
3. Pick out a country, learn about it, and pray for that country.
4. Walk around the block and pray for your neighbors.
5. Celebrate the anniversary of God answering a family prayer. For example, God saved Grandma from cancer last year. Lesson: Remembering past victories gives us hope in future struggles.
6. Form a circle and place pictures of a missionary family in the center. Then pray for them by name.

Listen – One thing parents forget to do is just listen to God. We would all agree that both our flesh and the enemy speak lies to us—*You're not smart. You can't do it. You're ugly. You're a bad kid*—and other lies. We can dismiss them as harmless or we can be intentional about teaching our kids how to "take every thought captive" (2 Cor. 10:5).

A simple practice is to have your children listen to God. Give them a simple question to repeat and then help them match it with God's character so they can learn to recognize truth. We want to teach them to battle lies like Jesus did—with the truth found in scripture—but first we need to help them recognize lies. Here's an example: "How do you feel about me, God?" If they "hear" something, you can ask if that sounds like something God would say. You should always preface your questions with the fact that whether or not they hear something is not the point and certainly doesn't make them better than anyone else. The point is to remember that God wants to talk with us, and we should honor Him by just "listening" from time to time. Having them listen helps them learn to practically understand that God loves to build up and not tear down. And it is always important to ask if they remembered a scripture during prayer. It highlights the fact that God's predominate way of speaking to us is through His word.

Tools Provided in This Book

....

34 Bible Stories with Questions and Answers Provided

After reading a story, it's useful to have prepared questions with answers so any parent can feel confident that they are drawing out key elements of the story. The questions and answers are intended to help teach the children, help them develop a more robust view of the story, and provide a solid foundation for understanding all the scriptures.

Bible Sound Off/Catechism (Three Provided)

To catechize means to instruct systematically, especially with questions, answers, explanations, and corrections. Therefore, a catechism is the manual or questions used to catechize someone. In order to avoid any negative connotations with the word *catechism*, we have chosen to simply call this tool Bible Sound Off. From early church history to the present day, this time-tested tool helps teach biblical truths that are vital for a good understanding of who God is and what His word says.

At first glance, it might seem that catechizing small children won't work, but it's amazing how much toddlers can absorb. In fact, the early years of development is when a parent wants to input as many facts as possible. As children develop, these facts become the well from which they draw when their brains develop reasoning.

Even with children as young as two or three, you can do one question per week and cover 52 questions in a year. You will be amazed at how they remember the answers and even more amazed at how you remember them. The best thing is that since you are the one reading the questions with the answers in front of you, you don't need to know anything. Many parents, including the author, have ended up catechizing themselves as they catechize their children.

You can research this more online. *Family Shepherds: Calling and Equipping Men to Lead Their Homes* by Voddie Baucham Jr. will show you how this could fit into family discipleship.

Scripture Blessings

These blessings are simply scriptures that have been somewhat personalized so a father, mother, grandparents, or even older siblings can pray them over children. This simple nightly ritual not only gives fathers and mothers the ability to pray scripture over their children, but it also creates the anticipation of being blessed by a parent each night. The common method is for the father or mother to place his or her hand on the head of each child and speak these blessings. In addition, these prayers can be used to teach a child to bless others such as siblings or even parents. You can have a different child pick the blessing each night and enjoy the look in their eyes as they try to find the perfect one. Children Desiring God has produced a tool called *A Father's Guide to Blessing His Children* that you can purchase to gain a Biblical understanding of a blessing. In fact, many of the blessings we provide are inspired by this resource, and some of them are the same. All credit to them for letting us ride on their coattails.

Song Recommendations

Children shouldn't be the only ones to sing to God and about God. They need to see their parents praise Him as well. The songs recommended are not any more foundational than other songs. But our hope is that your family will discover songs that become your family songs and that your children would see mom and dad model praising God in the home. A great idea is to find videos of these songs on the Internet so they can learn the melody.

Dictionary of Common Biblical Terms

These are very brief definitions that hopefully remain true to the Bible but are easy to understand.

Brief Summary of Old Testament Books for Reference or Memorization

These are simple, concise summaries that will give you quick insight into each book. As children get older, they might become good memory tools for knowing the Bible better.

Memory Passage Suggestions for Memorization

One thing I lament is that I was only taught single verses as a child. But childhood is the best time to learn chunks of scripture. Children's brains are not developed enough to reason and fully think through a devotional, but they can retain large amounts of information. Childhood is the best time to input as much as possible so as they age, they can grow from memorizing to working with the information and then to reasoning. Memorizing at an early age ensures that they have a deep well from which to draw.

Some tips: Use hand motions for each verse when possible. It makes it fun and also aids in memory. For instance, for "The LORD is my shepherd; I shall not want" (Ps. 23:1), simply point to the sky when you say *Lord* and point to yourself when you say *my*. It really is that simple. My kids have been learning Romans 8 for a while now, and we have motions for some of the verses and not for others. It isn't about having the perfect hand motions for each verse. It is about filling their minds with Bible passages that will be embedded in their hearts and minds. Just do what works for your family whether it's hand motions or memorizing each verse to a rhythm—anything that aids in memory.

Family Discipleship Bible Stories

1

Before "in the Beginning"

(Rev. 13:8; 1 Pet. 1:20; Eph. 1:4–5; Col. 1:17; Prov. 8:22–29)

The Bible begins with the phrase "in the beginning," but before "in the beginning," there was only God. There is one God—God the Father, God the Son, and God the Holy Spirit. God has always been, and He always will be. He is everlasting. That is what makes Him God. Nobody is like Him, and nobody thinks the way He does. God is also sovereign, which means He has the right, power, and authority to be in charge. Because He is sovereign, He does whatever pleases Him, and everything that pleases God is good. He is good not only because He creates good things and always loves in a good way, but because good is simply who He is. When we want to learn about God, we always have to remember that everything He does is good, and all His plans bring Him glory.

Before God made everything, He planned everything to the very last detail. God chose to create because it pleased Him. It made him happy to share His immense, perfect love with us. All of creation, every living thing, was designed, put together, and given life by God.

God chose to create man in His image, different from the animals. God already knew that men would never be perfect like He is and that they would need to be rescued. God planned and chose the people He would rescue even before

He made them. He chose them even before He made the world. He did that so His people would know they were His special creations, not because they were good or because they would do good things, but simply because it made Him happy to choose them. God even planned the way He would rescue them. He planned to send His son to die, be buried, and rise from the dead so He could rescue the ones He chose.

The Bible is God's word, and it tells us all about God, the story of His children, His creation, His enemies, and His Son. The Bible also tells us how God has good things planned for those who love Him and how everything will bring Him glory.

Just like the times when you have to trust that your parents want good things for you even when you don't understand or agree with them, there are times when you have to trust in God's goodness for you even when you don't understand what He is doing, God is still good and will bring great joy to those who trust Him. Remember, God has already made His plan, and His plan is good. And all of this was planned long ago, before "in the beginning."

Questions:

❝ Did God make His plan after man sinned or before?
  ◆ *God made a plan even before creation.*

❝ Why does God make the decisions He makes?
  ◆ *Because they bring Him glory.*

❝ Did God choose to rescue His children before or after creation?
  ◆ *God chose to rescue His children before He even made them.*

2

The Creation of the World

(Genesis 1–2)

In the beginning, before there was anything we see today, there was God. God was all there was. There is One God—God the Father, God the Son, and God the Holy Spirit.

"And God said, 'Let there be light,' and there was light" (Gen. 1:3). Just like that, light shined out of the darkness, and something came from nothing. In the same way, God created air and water, the land and the seas, the sun, moon, and stars, the birds of the sky, the fish of the sea, land animals, and man.

Everything we see today was created out of an overflow of the love between God the Father, God the Son, and God the Holy Spirit. In six days, God created everything. He made animals to fly above the water and the land. He made ducks, ravens, doves, eagles, and robins. He made the animals that live in the water—lobsters, snails, sharks, whales, dolphins, and so many colorful fish that we can't even count them all. He also made land animals—tigers, elephants, monkeys, giraffes, dogs, cats, and even the mighty lion.

But God saved his best work for last. He said, "Let us make man in our image, after our likeness" (Gen. 1:26). And God created the first man, Adam, out of the dirt of the earth. Out of the first man's rib, God made the first woman, Eve. She was given to Adam as a helper. Adam was to protect her and love her because she was needed to help him carry out God's plan. God made man to rule over all living things and told him to be fruitful and multiply.

God placed Adam and Eve in a perfect garden and gave them everything they needed. And best of all, God gave them Himself. Adam and Eve lived in God's presence. They could walk in the garden with God and enjoy all of His creation.

Among all the plants and trees in the garden, were the tree of life and the tree of the knowledge of good and evil. God gave Adam specific instructions not to

eat from the tree of the knowledge of good and evil. If he did, he would die. All Adam had to do was trust God, enjoy His creation, and give Him glory by obeying His commands.

God looked over everything He had made and said it was good. The next day, the seventh day, God rested and called it holy.

Questions:

❝ What did God make everything out of?
  ◇ *Nothing.*

❝ What did God make Adam and Eve out of?
  ◇ *He made Adam out of the dirt and made Eve out of Adam's rib.*

❝ Whom did God tell not to eat from the tree of the knowledge of good and evil—Adam or Eve?
  ◇ *God told Adam.*

3

The Creation of the Spirit World

(Gen. 1:1; Job 38:4–7; Ps. 8; Isa. 14:12–15; Ezek. 28:11–19; Luke 10:18; Rev. 12:1–9)

When God created the heavens and the earth, the angels were already there. God created them to fulfill His purposes. When the angels saw God's great power, beauty, and creativity, they sang together and shouted for joy, giving glory and praise to God the most high.

There was one angel whose name was Lucifer, which means bright morning star. He was the leader of the angels. When he saw the praise the other angels gave to God, he became jealous. Lucifer decided in his heart that he would raise his throne above the throne of God and be like God. Lucifer then set out to trick the other angels and convince them to worship him instead. A third of all the angels began to follow Lucifer instead of the one true God.

But God knows everything. He knew what Lucifer was thinking and doing. Lucifer may have thought he was being sneaky, but nothing can be hidden from God. So God judged Lucifer and the angels he had tricked. He drove them out of heaven and said that one day he would punish Lucifer and the fallen angels. God changed Lucifer's name to Satan, and the fallen angels were called demons. Satan is also called the serpent or the deceiver.

To this day, Satan continues to lead his demons in a rebellion against God. They are the enemies of God. Satan and his demons roam about the earth trying to trick people so they will follow Satan instead of loving, trusting, and obeying God. But because God is all-knowing and all-powerful, we never have to fear His enemies. We can trust God, knowing that He is good. Nothing can be hidden from Him, and nothing can stop His plans.

Questions:

❝ What were angels created to do?
- ✧ *To serve the purposes of God.*

❝ What do the rebellious angels (demons) do?
- ✧ *Try to trick people to follow Satan instead of God.*

❝ Should we ever be afraid of demons and their work?
- ✧ *No. God is good, all-knowing, and all-powerful. Nothing can stop His plan.*

4

The Fall of Man

(Genesis 3)

Remember when God placed Adam and Eve in the perfect garden that He had created and told them they could eat from any tree of the garden except the tree of the knowledge of good and evil? One day as Adam and Eve were in the garden, a snake, which was really Satan, the deceiver, came to them. The snake asked Eve, "Did God actually say, 'You shall not eat of any tree in the garden'?" (Gen. 3:1). Even though Adam—the one who had heard directly from God that he could eat of any tree except one—was there, too, he was silent and let Eve answer. Eve said, "We may eat of the fruit of the trees in the garden, but God said, 'You shall not eat of the fruit of the tree that is in the midst of the garden, neither shall you touch it, lest you die'" (Gen. 3:2–3).

But that is not what God said. Adam failed to honor and obey God by correcting Eve or by telling the snake the truth. The snake then tempted Eve with a lie, telling her that eating the fruit from the tree of the knowledge of good and evil would make her just like God, and that this was the real reason God had forbidden it. Being tricked, she held the fruit in her hands and took a bite. Then she gave some to Adam, and he ate it, too.

In that moment, everything changed. All of a sudden, Adam and Eve saw everything differently. They realized that they were naked and had been naked ever since God created them. Up until that point, they had been unashamed because they constantly felt God's great love for them. Eating the fruit changed everything. Now, they were ashamed and tried to hide themselves from God. But remember, God knows everything. So, God went looking for them in the garden and called to Adam, "Where are you?" (Gen. 3:9). Adam answered and said, "I heard the sound of you in the garden, and I was afraid, because I was naked, and I hid myself" (Gen. 3:10). Because of His great love, God was giving Adam a chance to tell the truth. But Adam chose not to do that. He even blamed God because He was the one who gave him Eve.

Eve was deceived, but Adam is the one who was responsible. Adam sinned. Sin is any thought, action, or attitude that does not bring glory to God. As a result of Adam's sin, God cursed the snake and the ground, and drove Adam and Eve from the garden. But that was not the end the story. God was already doing something amazing that Adam and Eve could not understand. Even as He drove them from the garden, He mysteriously pronounced that one day a man like Adam, born of a woman, would crush the snake, sin, and death. And all things would be good, just like in the beginning.

Questions:

❝ Was Adam or Eve responsible for bringing sin and death into the world, and why?
  ✧ *Adam was responsible because he was the one God gave the instructions to, not Eve.*

❝ Was Adam with Eve when she was deceived by the snake?
  ✧ *Yes, Adam was with Eve in the garden.*

❝ Who do you think the man like Adam is that God said would one day crush the snake?
  ✧ *Jesus (God the Son).*

5

The Story of Job

(Job 1–42)

There lived in the land of Uz a righteous man named Job. He had 10 children, and he was very wealthy. But Job did not let wealth distract him from fearing God. So Job stayed away from evil.

One day the angels came before God. Satan, who had been roaming about the earth, also joined them. God pointed out Job, how he was a blameless and upright man who feared God and turned away from evil. Satan said that was only because God had protected Job, blessed his work, and given him great wealth. Satan argued that if God allowed Job's possessions to be taken away, Job would curse God. God allowed Satan to take Job's possessions, but forbade him from harming Job's body.

Satan destroyed all of Job's wealth and even killed all 10 of his children. However, Job remained faithful to God. He said, "The Lord gave, and the Lord has taken away; blessed be the name of the Lord" (Job 1:21).

So Satan returned before God. Once again, God pointed out Job and declared that he stayed faithful even though he had suffered the loss of all his children and possessions. Satan said that Job would surely curse God if his body became sick and he had to suffer physical pain. God then allowed Satan to bring disease on Job but said he could not kill him.

Satan struck Job with horrible sores from the bottom of his feet to the top of his head. Once Satan did this, Job's friends accused him of doing evil. Even his wife told him to curse God and die. But Job still did not curse God and sin. Job had three friends who were convinced that Job's suffering was God's punishment for something he did. They could not believe that God would allow a righteous man to suffer so much.

Again and again throughout his suffering, Job begged God to talk with him. Finally, God granted Job's request and began thundering questions at Job that were impossible for him to answer. Each question was a reminder that God is far greater and wiser than any man. God's overpowering questions humbled Job and, more importantly, changed him. Job said that before his time of suffering,

The Story of Job

he had only heard of God. But after this encounter, he felt as if he had truly seen God. In the end, God restored Job to even greater blessings than before. The greatest blessing was that Job now knew God better.

Questions:

❝ Could Satan strike Job without God's permission?
 ◇ *No. Satan could only strike Job or his possessions with God's permission.*

❝ What happened when God finally answered Job and started asking him questions?
 ◇ *Job was humbled and realized that God is far wiser than man.*

❝ Do you think that in the end Job was glad or sad that he went through suffering?
 ◇ *He was glad because it helped him know God better.*

6

The Flood: Part 1

(Genesis 6–7)

After Adam sinned and was sent out of the garden, everything began to change. Sin became part of everyone who lived, and death came to all creation. People made pretend gods instead of serving the one true God. God's heart was sad because of all the sin in the world. He had created everything good, and now, because of Adam's sin, wickedness was everywhere. God was so sad that He decided to destroy everyone on earth, including all the animals, birds, and plants.

But there was one man who was not like everyone else. His name was Noah. He was a good man who pleased God. So God invited Noah into His plan. God told Noah to build a huge boat called an ark because He was going to make it rain so much that the whole world would flood. Because God loves all His creation, He told Noah to gather the animals two by two and bring them onto the ark. God promised Noah that if he would follow His instructions, build the ark, and bring the animals inside of it, Noah and all his family would be saved from the coming flood.

But when God told Noah to build the boat, it had never rained on the earth. Can you imagine what it would be like to build a boat when there is no water around? God was asking Noah to trust Him even though everyone would make fun of him.

So day after day, year after year, Noah slowly built the ark. Noah waited and trusted God for 120 years. Then, drip, drip, drip. It finally started to rain.

Noah had done everything God asked. He built the ark and loaded the animals. Then, God closed the door, and Noah and his family watched as the rains came down. Rain started pouring so quickly that the desert soon became a lake. After 40 days and 40 nights of unbelievable storms, the entire earth was flooded. All the

The Flood: Part 1

people who were once on earth were now gone, wiped away by God's powerful flood. All the trees and mountains—*everything*—were under water. But even though God destroyed everything, He kept his promise and saved Noah and his family.

Questions:

❝ Why did everyone on earth change, and what happened to all of creation?
  ◆ *Because of Adam's disobedience, sin became part of everyone, and death came to all creation.*

❝ Why did Noah build a boat where there was no water?
  ◆ *Because he trusted God that by building a boat, his family would be saved.*

❝ What promises did God keep in the flood story?
  ◆ *That He would destroy all creation and that He would save Noah's family.*

7

The Flood: Part 2

(Genesis 8–9)

Noah was God's friend when all other people had turned from God. In fact, man was so wicked that God destroyed not only man, but also all of His creation. God told Noah to build an ark, gather two of each animal, and take his family into the ark because He was going to flood the earth. God is faithful and did everything He said He would do. He saved Noah's family and the animals on the ark while He flooded the earth and destroyed all of creation outside the ark.

After 150 days, God caused the water to go down, and the ark landed on the mountains of Ararat. A few months later, Noah sent a dove to see if the waters on earth had dried up. But the dove didn't find anywhere to land and returned to the ark. Noah waited seven more days and sent the dove out again. This time, the dove came back with an olive leaf, so Noah knew that the earth was dry. Seven days later, Noah sent another dove out, and it did not return. Noah then knew that the earth was ready for his family and the animals to leave the ark.

Noah and his family stepped off the ark and unloaded all the animals. The first thing Noah and his family did on dry ground was worship the Lord. Noah built an altar and sacrificed some of the animals to God as a way to show God how much he loved and trusted Him. God then made a secure, unbreakable promise with

Noah called a covenant. God could do that because He is completely trustworthy. God's covenant promise was that He would never again destroy man or every living creature with a flood because of man's wickedness.

What God did next is something we still see today. He placed a rainbow in the sky as a sign of His promise. The great thing is that the rainbow doesn't just remind us of God's promise. God sees it and remembers His promise, too. Today, people are just as wicked as they were during Noah's time. This makes God sad because of His great love for His creation. But because of His promise, He will never destroy us again with a flood. God always keeps His promises. Remember that the next time you see a rainbow in the sky.

The Flood: Part 2

Questions:

❝ What is the strongest, most secure promise called?
  ◆ *A covenant.*

❝ Why can a covenant made by God never be broken?
  ◆ *Because God is completely trustworthy.*

❝ Is there any situation where God might destroy the earth again with a flood?
  ◆ *No. God will never do that again.*

8

Tower of Babel: God Knows Everything

(Genesis 11:1–9)

At one time, the whole world had just one language. That made life easy for everyone. But people sinned and tried to make themselves famous instead of giving glory to God. God knows all things and has planned things out from the beginning, so He already knew how He would use this situation to bring Himself the glory He deserves.

In their sin, the people of the earth said to one another, "Come, let us build ourselves a city and a tower with its top in the heavens, and let us make a name for ourselves, lest we be dispersed over the face of the whole earth" (Gen. 11:4).

The Lord God came down from heaven to see what man was doing. Now God is everywhere all the time, but this is a way of telling us that God lowers Himself to our level at times. When God saw what the people were doing, He said:

> Behold, they are one people, and they have all one language, and this is only the beginning of what they will do. And nothing that they propose to do will now be impossible for them. Come, let us go down and there confuse their language, so that they may not understand one another's speech.
>
> —Gen. 11:6–7

So God confused their language and scattered the people all over the world.

When God gave the people different languages, everything changed. All of a sudden, they couldn't understand each other. Instead of being one people, they were all different. When we can't understand someone today, we say they are babbling. The tower that the people were building was named the Tower of Babel because once God confused their language, they could not understand each other.

Remember, God knows everything, so He knew that eventually He would rescue people from every nation and they would worship Him together. But in order to do this, people would have to be scattered all over the earth and speak different languages. Instead of doing it at the beginning of creation, He waited until the right people gathered in the wrong way. That is why people from different nations are so important to God. It is also why we don't judge people because their skin is a different color or they speak a different language. God made people look and talk in different ways because one day He will be praised by every nation and tongue. He will adopt people from all over the world to be His children. Adoption is when someone is specially chosen to be part of a family. It is a wonderful thing to be adopted, and it is a big part of God's master design.

Tower of Babel: God Knows Everything

❝ Questions:

❝ Why did the people want to build a tower?
  ✧ *So they could build a name for themselves and not be scattered.*

❝ What did God do when the people decided to make a name for themselves?
  ✧ *He gave them different languages that confused them, and then He scattered them all over the world.*

❝ How was creating different people with different languages part of God's plan?
  ✧ *It was part of His plan to one day be worshiped by every nation and every language.*

9

Abraham and Isaac: God Is Faithful

(Genesis 12–22)

There once was a man named Abram. One day God said to him, "Go from your country and your kindred and your father's house to the land that I will show you" (Gen. 12:1). The Lord also told Abram that in him, all the families of the earth would be blessed. Abram heard this message when he was 75 years old. Abram said, "Behold, you have given me no offspring, and a member of my household will be my heir" (Gen. 15:3). But God told him to look outside and try to count the stars. Then God told him that he would one day have as many children as there are stars. Abram believed this, and God considered his belief as righteousness. Being righteous or blameless makes you pleasing to God. Isn't that crazy that all you have to do to please God is *believe* God? Abram didn't have to do anything except trust what God said. So Abram packed up and went to the land God showed him.

God is so powerful that He even told Abram in a dream that one day his offspring would be slaves in a land but that He would deliver them. And guess what? One day this happened just like God said. God always keeps His word. He is so awesome that even today He speaks where we can hear it—in the Bible, in dreams, in visions, or quietly to our hearts—telling us things He wants us to know.

Abram's wife was named Sarai. Instead of waiting for God to fulfill His promise, Sarai came up with her own plan. It is sad, because just like Adam, Abram listened to his wife instead of God. Because she was too old to have children, she told Abram to have a child with her servant Hagar. Hagar gave birth to a boy named Ishmael, but he was not the son the Lord promised. When Abram was 99 years old, God spoke and told him that He would soon fulfill His promise. God then changed Abram's name to Abraham, which means father of a multitude. The Lord also changed Sarai's name to Sarah, which means princess.

It was incredible that Abraham believed God since Sarah was now 99 years old. Abraham asked why God wouldn't just use Ishmael. But God said, "No, but Sarah your wife shall bear you a son, and you shall call his name Isaac. I will establish my covenant with him as an everlasting covenant for his offspring after him" (Gen. 17:19). Once again, Abraham believed what God said.

A year later, Sarah gave birth to a child, just as God promised, and they named him Isaac. In his old age, Abraham loved Isaac very much. Isaac was the son of the promise.

Questions:

❝ Why did God consider Abraham righteous?
  ◆ *Abraham believed and trusted God.*

❝ What did God say would one day happen to Abraham's descendants?
  ◆ *They would be slaves, but God would deliver them from slavery.*

❝ Abraham had two sons, Ishmael and Isaac. Which one was the son of promise?
  ◆ *Isaac was the son of promise.*

10

Ishmael's Story

(Genesis 16–21)

Isaac was the son of promise. But what about the other little boy, Ishmael? Remember, Abraham's wife Sarah had a hard time waiting for God and decided to help God. But God doesn't need help from anyone to make His promises come true. Instead of waiting for God, Sarah came up with a plan to try to help God.

Just like Adam did in the garden, Abraham listened to his wife instead of listening to God. The result is that Abraham disobeyed God and used Sarah's plan. Sarah had a slave named Hagar who was young enough to have children. She gave Hagar to Abraham, and Hagar had his child—Ishmael. The only problem is that it was not God's plan. But the wonderful thing about God is that that even when we disobey, He still shows His great love for us.

When Isaac was born, Sarah wanted Ishmael to go away. God told Abraham to do what Sarah wanted and send Hagar and Ishmael away. This was hard for Abraham because he loved both his sons, but he told Hagar and Ishmael to leave. As they wandered through the desert, they ran out of water, and Hagar left Ishmael under some bushes because she could not bear to watch him die. An angel of God appeared and told Hagar to take Ishmael by the hand because God was going to make him into a great nation. Then God opened her eyes, and she saw a well of water that would provide what they needed to survive. God continued to be with Ishmael, and when he grew up, his family did become a great nation. But God also declared that Ishmael and his descendants would be against everyone, and everyone would be against them.

So God showed His goodness to Abraham by taking care of his firstborn son, Ishmael. God is good to us that way, even when we disobey Him. Even though Ishmael wasn't the son of promise, Ishmael's family became a great nation. But Abraham knew the blessing would come through Isaac and that through his family, the whole world would be blessed.

Questions:

❝ How was Abraham like Adam, the first man God created?
  ✧ *Just like Adam, Abraham listened to his wife instead of God.*

❝ Was Ishmael's mother Abraham's wife?
  ✧ *No, Ishmael's mother was a slave woman named Hagar.*

❝ God made Ishmael's descendants a great nation, but was he the son God promised Abraham?
  ✧ *No, Isaac was the son of promise.*

11

Isaac and the Promise

(Genesis 22)

Abraham was 100 years old when his wife, Sarah, gave birth to a son. God had told Abraham that his descendants from that son would be as numerous as the stars in the sky. Abraham must have been pleased when his son was born because God's plan was actually coming true. He named that son Isaac. Then, one day the Lord did something that sounds crazy.

God tested Abraham. He told him to sacrifice Isaac. Back then, people who didn't follow the real God made a sacrifice by taking an animal, cutting it up, and burning it on an altar. This was a way of keeping a good relationship with their pretend gods. But people who followed the real God made a sacrifice in the same way but for a different reason. They offered a sacrifice because they loved God and wanted to show Him that He was more valuable than anything they had.

The people who loved God always sacrificed animals, never people. People, who are made in the image of God, are His special, treasured creation. So when God asked Abraham to sacrifice Isaac, it was unlike anything God had ever asked anyone before. You would think Abraham would question God, but instead, he simply trusted that God knew best. Early one morning, Abraham took Isaac, along with some wood, and went to Mount Moriah where God told him to sacrifice Isaac.

As they went up the mountain, Isaac asked where the lamb was for the sacrifice. Abraham said, "God will provide for himself the lamb for a burnt offering, my son" (Gen. 22:8). When they got to the place God told him to go, Abraham built an altar, tied up his son, and laid him on top of the wood. Wait! Is Abraham going to kill his beloved son, the son of promise? How will he have descendants if he kills his son?

Those are great questions. But remember, Abraham learned to trust God no matter what. Abraham took a knife, raised it high, and was about to sacrifice his son. Just then, an angel of the Lord said, "Abraham, Abraham! . . . Do not lay your hand on the boy or do anything to him, for now I know that you fear God, seeing you have not withheld your son, your only son, from me" (Gen. 22:11–12). As Abraham looked up, he saw a ram caught in some bushes. He took the ram and sacrificed it instead of his son. The angel told him:

> Because you have done this and have not withheld your son, your only son, I will surely bless you, and I will surely multiply your offspring as the stars of heaven and as the sand that is on the seashore.
>
> —Gen. 22:16–17

God tested Abraham, and he passed the test.

Questions:

❝ Why did people who followed the one true God never sacrifice a person?
   ◆ *Because people are made in the image of God.*

❝ When Isaac asked where the sacrifice was, what did Abraham tell him?
   ◆ *That God would provide the sacrifice.*

❝ What did Abraham sacrifice instead of his son Isaac?
   ◆ *God provided a ram as a substitute.*

12

Joseph: Part 1

(Genesis 37–40)

Abraham's son, Isaac, married Rebecca. Isaac and Rebecca had twin boys, Esau and Jacob. God was at work directing which family member He would use for His purposes. So before the twins were born, even though Esau was older and would have received the firstborn blessing, God said the older would serve the younger. That meant Jacob's family line would be used to fulfill God's promise to Abraham. Jacob discovered who God is through his own life experiences, and God changed his name to Israel, which means "one who wrestles with God." Jacob eventually had sons who would all be part of God's plan. One of them—Joseph, the son of his old age—Jacob loved more than the others. Because of his great love for Joseph, Jacob made him a beautiful, colorful robe. This gift made Joseph's brothers jealous. In fact, they were more than jealous; they were angry.

God speaks in a number of ways. He mainly speaks through His word, but there are also times when He talks through dreams. God talked that way to Joseph. But when Joseph told the dreams to his family, they got very angry. That is because in Joseph's dreams, he would rule over his brothers in the future. In the first dream, Joseph and his brothers were in the field tying up bundles of grain in sheaves. Joseph's sheaf rose up, and his brothers' sheaves bowed down to his. His brothers questioned him right away and said, "Are you indeed to rule over us?" (Gen. 37:8). They began to hate Joseph and wanted to get rid of him.

In the second dream, Joseph's brothers were eleven stars, and his father and mother were the sun and moon. The eleven stars and the sun and moon were all bowing down to Joseph. When Joseph told his dream, his father said, "Shall I and your mother and your brothers indeed come to bow ourselves to the ground before you?" (Gen. 37:10). The brothers were still jealous of him, and his father remembered what Joseph said.

Sometime later, Jacob sent Joseph to check on his brothers as they were out shepherding the flocks. The brothers saw him coming and decided to kill him. When Joseph arrived, they stripped him of his beautiful robe, tore it, dipped it in blood, and told their father that a fierce animal killed Joseph. But Joseph wasn't dead. Instead of killing Joseph, they sold him as a slave to some Ishmaelites headed to Egypt for 20 pieces of silver. Then he was sold again in Egypt to an officer of Pharaoh named Potiphar. Can you believe it? Joseph's own brothers betrayed him and sold him for money.

Joseph: Part 1

That wasn't the last time Joseph would be treated unfairly. But God was with Joseph, and he rose to power in Potiphar's house. Sadly, one day Potiphar's wife made up lies about Joseph, and he was sent to prison. Once again, because God was with Joseph, he also rose to power in prison. While in prison and with God's help, Joseph explained another prisoner's dream. Soon after, that man was released. But instead of helping Joseph get out, the man forgot about Joseph. Once again, Joseph was betrayed. Jacob's favorite son's only hope was to continue to trust the one true God.

Questions:

❝ How did God speak to Joseph?
   ✧ *He spoke to Joseph through dreams.*

❝ Joseph's brothers sold him, but what did they tell Jacob (Israel), their father?
   ✧ *They told Jacob (Israel) that fierce animals killed him.*

❝ Why did Joseph rise to power in Potiphar's house and in prison?
   ✧ *Because God was with him.*

13

Joseph: Part 2

(Genesis 41–46)

Joseph was one of Abraham's great-grandsons. He was sold into slavery by his jealous brothers and ended up in an Egyptian prison because of lies told about him. One day, Pharaoh, the ruler of Egypt, had dreams that he wanted to understand because he couldn't stop thinking about them. But none of Pharaoh's magicians could explain what the dreams meant. Even today, God still speaks in dreams, but usually, just like Pharaoh, we need someone to help us understand them. In God's wisdom, he chose to speak in a dream to Pharaoh, even though he was not one of his chosen people and worshiped pretend gods.

But since God was the one who gave Pharaoh the dream, He already had a plan for who was going to help. Earlier, while Joseph was in prison, God helped him explain another man's dreams. That man now worked for Pharaoh, so he told Pharaoh about this man named Joseph who could explain his dream. Standing in front of Pharaoh, Joseph let him know that he wasn't able to do it on his own. It was only through God's strength that he could give the meaning of the dream. Once again, Joseph trusted God, and God told him what the dream meant. Joseph explained to Pharaoh that a famine was coming and that he should make preparations to store up extra food before the famine came. Pharaoh was so pleased that he made Joseph second in command of all of Egypt. And then, just like God said in the dream, a famine came upon the land.

People were coming from everywhere to buy food from Egypt. One day, Joseph's jealous brothers who sold him into slavery came to Egypt to buy food. They didn't recognize Joseph when they were bowing down to ask to buy food, but Joseph recognized them. The dream God had given Joseph years ago came true just like God said: His family bowed before him.

Now was Joseph's chance to get even, right? God gave him the power to punish them, right? No! Instead, after putting them through some trials, Joseph showed great love for his family. He told them that even though they tried to harm him, God used their jealousy to send him ahead of them to save his family. God promised to make the families of Abraham, Isaac, and Jacob great, and God always keeps his promises.

God used Joseph's jealous brothers to send Israel's family to Egypt so they would survive the famine. But Egypt is also the place where they would eventually be enslaved, just like God told Abraham.

Joseph forgave his brothers and was reunited with his father. He also met his newest brother, Benjamin. Even though Joseph went through tough times, God was with him, and now his family was safe in Egypt and treated well by the Pharaoh because of Joseph. They were given the best of the land to shepherd their flocks, and they multiplied greatly.

Questions:

❝ God gave Pharaoh a dream, but did he serve the one true God?
- *No, Pharaoh worshipped many false gods.*

❝ Who did Joseph say would give the meaning of the dream?
- *He said God would give the meaning of the dream.*

❝ How did God use Joseph's brothers to help fulfill his promises to Abraham?
- *God used their jealousy to send him to Egypt so he could save his family.*

14

Moses: Part 1

(Exodus 1–2)

The Jewish people, the family of God's promise, grew extremely large in Egypt. And just as God promised Abraham, they were afflicted for 400 years. God also promised the people of Israel a land of their own. Now it was time for God to move them from Egypt to the land He promised Abraham long ago. But 400 years is a long time, so long that the new ruler of Egypt had made slaves of God's chosen family—the Jews, who are also called Hebrews or Israelites. This new Pharaoh depended on them for slave work, but he was also scared because the Israelites multiplied greatly and he feared they might challenge his power. There was also talk of one who would one day rescue the Hebrew people, a deliverer. So Pharaoh decided to kill all the new Hebrew babies who were boys. He thought that would take care of the problem.

One of the Hebrew mothers saw that her son was a fine child, so she hid him so he would not be killed. Soon, she couldn't hide him anymore, so she put him in a basket and placed him in the river. Pharaoh's daughter was taking a bath in that same river. She found the baby crying and felt sorry for him. She adopted the baby into her family. (Adoption is when a child doesn't have anyone to take care of her or him, and other parents step in to rescue them, and they become a new family.) As that baby grew up, Pharaoh's daughter treated him just like her biological son.

She named him Moses because she drew him out of the water, and Moses sounds like the Hebrew word that means "to draw out."

Even though Moses was raised in Pharaoh's household, he grew up to be concerned for his people and went to watch them doing their hard labor. One day, as a grown man, he saw an Egyptian beating one of the Hebrew slaves. After making sure no one was looking, Moses killed the Egyptian and hid his body in the sand. The next day, Moses saw two Hebrew men arguing and asked why they were quarreling. One of the men asked, "Who made you a prince and a judge over us? Do you mean to kill me as you killed the Egyptian?" (Exod. 2:14). Then Moses was afraid because he thought, "Surely the thing is known" (Exod. 2:14). And just as Moses feared, when Pharaoh found out, he sought to kill Moses.

So Moses ran from Egypt to the land of Midian. There he settled and married a woman named Zipporah. She gave him a son, but since Moses still felt like a foreigner in a foreign land, he named his son Gershom, which sounds like the Hebrew word for "foreigner." But back in Egypt, the Hebrew people were still being treated badly, and they cried out to God, begging to be rescued. They prayed that God would remember His covenant with Abraham, with Isaac, and with Jacob.

Moses: Part 1

Questions:

❝ What is the word we use when God provides a family for a child who has nobody to care for him or her?
  ◇ *Adoption*

❝ Did Moses grow up as a Hebrew or as an Egyptian?
  ◇ *Moses grew up as an Egyptian, the adopted son of Pharaoh's daughter.*

❝ What did the Hebrews do in hopes of being rescued?
  ◇ *They cried out to God, asking Him to remember His covenant with Abraham, Isaac, and Jacob.*

15

Moses: Part 2

(Exodus 3–11)

God moved the Jewish people to Egypt to save them from a great famine. Because of Abraham's great-great grandson Joseph, they experienced great favor for a while. But in time, a new Pharaoh came to power and enslaved God's people. He tried to kill all the male Hebrew babies in hopes of keeping them from growing too powerful. One Hebrew mother put her boy into a basket in the river in hopes of saving him. He was found and eventually adopted by Pharaoh's daughter, who named him Moses, and he grew up in the household of Pharaoh. After killing an Egyptian, Moses fled to Midian, where he got married and shepherded his father-in-law's sheep.

One day, while watching the flock, the angel of the Lord appeared to Moses in a bush that was burning but not being consumed. This definitely got Moses's attention. It was there that God spoke to him and said:

> I have surely seen the affliction of my people who are in Egypt and have heard their cry because of their taskmasters. I know their sufferings, and I have come down to deliver them out of the hand of the Egyptians and to bring them up out of that land to a good and broad land.
>
> —Exod. 3:7–8

Moses quickly asked, "Who am I that I should go to Pharaoh and bring the children of Israel out of Egypt?" God told Moses, "I will be with you." Moses said, "If I come to the people of Israel and say to them, 'The God of your fathers has sent me to you,' and they ask me, 'What is his name?' what shall I say to them?" God said, "I AM WHO I AM. . . . This is my name forever, and thus I am to be remembered throughout all generations" (Exod. 3:11–15).

So Moses and his brother Aaron went to Pharaoh and said, "Thus says the LORD, Israel is my firstborn son, and I say to you, 'Let my son go that he may serve me.' If you refuse to let him go, behold, I will kill your firstborn son" (Exod. 4:22–23). Pharaoh later said, "Who is the LORD that I should obey his voice?" (Exod. 5:2). Pharaoh told them to prove themselves by a miracle, so Aaron threw down his staff, and it became a serpent. But Pharaoh's magicians did the same. Then Aaron's staff swallowed up the other serpents showing that the LORD is more powerful. Pharaoh still would not listen. Then Moses told him God would send plagues. First God turned the water into blood. Then He sent frogs, gnats, and flies. He killed the cows, gave the people boils, and sent hail, locusts, and darkness. Each plague showed that God is the one true God and that the Egyptian gods were fake. God protected his people from the plagues, but even that did not convince Pharaoh to let Israel go.

Finally, God told Moses that after one more plague, Pharaoh would let Israel go. Moses told Pharaoh that at midnight, the Angel of Death would pass through Egypt, and every firstborn in the land would die. Moses, Aaron, and all the Hebrews living in Egypt had children who might die, but God always has a plan for His people. The plan would not only save God's chosen people, but it would point to the ultimate sacrifice God would eventually make many years later.

Moses: Part 2

~~~~~~~~~~~~~~~~~~~~~~ **Questions:** ~~~~~~~~~~~~~~~~~~~~~~

❝ How did God speak to Moses?
   ◇ *The angel of the Lord appeared to him in flames from a burning bush.*

❝ What is the name God told Moses to call him?
   ◇ *I AM WHO I AM*

❝ Pharaoh wouldn't let God's people go, so how did God respond?
   ◇ *He kept sending powerful plagues upon only the Egyptians.*

~~~~~~

16

Passover

(Exodus 12)

On the night of the final plague, God told Moses how the Hebrews could ensure that death passed over their homes. He would protect their firstborn from death. That night, God was going to go into all the land of Egypt and kill the firstborn of all Egypt, even the firstborn cattle. Plague after plague, Pharaoh told God he would not let God's people go. On that night, God would show that He was the one whose power and wisdom is above all people. God is the one who sent His chosen people to Egypt for the purpose of delivering them according to His special plan. God is the one who raises up people, rulers, and nations, and He is the one who lowers people, rulers, and nations according to His purposes.

So on Passover, God's people were to take an unblemished lamb and kill it, just like God told them. They were then to take some of the blood and put it on the doorposts of their houses. Then after they roasted the lamb, they were to dress up as if they were ready to leave and eat the lamb. All the Israelites did just as Moses told them. That night, on Passover, God passed through the land and killed all the firstborn in Egypt. But wherever He saw the lamb's blood on the doorposts, He passed over those homes and kept the firstborn inside safe from death. Every Egyptian family lost their firstborn that night. The Egyptians' cries were heard throughout the land, but the Israelites were kept safe.

Each year on that same day, God's chosen people have remembered the Passover throughout the generations. When the children born many years after that night celebrate Passover, they are told of God's awesome power and how He struck down the Egyptians but passed over His people, saving the firstborn from death. The story reminds them of the bitterness of slavery and how God's mighty hand delivered them, punished all of Egypt, and gave life to a new nation. The story is a shadow of another unblemished sacrifice whose blood would one day cover and cleanse people from a death they deserve.

Passover

Questions:

❝ God sent 10 plagues on Egypt. What was the last plague?
  ◆ *Death of the firstborn in each family.*

❝ What did the Israelites have to do in order to be protected from the final plague?
  ◆ *Place the blood of an unblemished lamb on the doorposts of their house.*

❝ Why did God tell the Israelites to celebrate Passover every year?
  ◆ *To remind them of the bitterness of slavery and how God delivered them.*

17

Deliverance from Egypt

(Exodus 12–14)

Finally, after the 10th plague that ended in the death of the firstborn of every Egyptian family and even the firstborn of the cattle, Pharaoh told Moses that Israel should go. As the people of God left, they followed Moses's instructions and asked the Egyptians for gold, jewelry, and clothing. This was all according to God's plan, so they left with these things. God would give them a chance to serve Him with that wealth later, but on this day they got to see how God's plans are always for His glory. After many years in Egypt, a nation was being born. The people were free from slavery and on their way to a land promised by the creator of all things.

God led the Hebrews out of Egypt by a pillar of cloud by day and a pillar of fire by night. Knowing His people would be fearful if they took the quickest route, God led them toward the Red Sea. God would show them one more time just how powerful He was compared to the Pharaoh who had controlled them for so long. Pharaoh thought they were lost and wandering, so he decided to pursue them. But God had made a different plan.

As Pharaoh drew near, the people of God grew fearful and cried out to the Lord. Moses told them not to fear and to stand firm and see the salvation of the Lord. God commanded Moses to lift up his staff and stretched it over the sea. God sent a strong east wind that divided the waters, and they became a wall on each side. This miracle allowed the Hebrews to pass through the Red Sea on dry land. Because God placed His pillar of fire behind the Jewish people, Pharaoh could not pursue them until God allowed it. Once Israel was safely on the other side, God let the Egyptians go after them. God commanded Moses to lift up his staff again, and this time, the waters crashed back down on the Egyptians. That day Israel witnessed God's great power and saw the Egyptians dead on the seashore. That day, Israel feared the Lord.

Deliverance from Egypt

～ **Questions:** ～

❝ What did the Hebrews do before they left Egypt?
  ◆ *They plundered the Egyptians by asking for and receiving gold, jewelry, and fine clothing.*

❝ How did God lead the Hebrews once they left Egypt?
  ◆ *By a pillar of cloud by day and a pillar of fire by night.*

❝ What was God's plan in this entire story?
  ◆ *To get glory and so all of Egypt would know that there is only one God.*

18

The Ten Commandments

(Exodus 19–20)

After walking in the wilderness of Sinai for three months, God had His people camp at Mt. Sinai. There, God instructed Moses to tell Israel that if they would obey His voice and keep His covenant, Israel would be God's treasured possession among all peoples, a kingdom of priests and a holy nation. All the people answered together, "All that the Lord has spoken we will do" (Exod. 19:7). God told Moses to tell the people to get ready, for in three days He would come down in the sight of all the people. The people were not to go near the mountain. If they even touched it, they would die.

So on the third day, just like He said, God came down to the mountain. There was thunder and lightning, a thick cloud of smoke, and a very loud trumpet. All that caused the people to tremble. God said:

> I am the Lord your God, who brought you out of the land of Egypt, out of the house of slavery. You shall have no other gods before me You shall not make for yourself a carved image. . . . You shall not take the name of the Lord your God in vain. . . . Remember the Sabbath day, to keep it holy. . . . Honor your father and your mother, that your days may be long in the land that the Lord your God is giving you. . . . You shall not murder. You shall

not commit adultery. You shall not steal. You shall not bear false witness against your neighbor. You shall not covet your neighbor's house; you shall not covet your neighbor's wife . . . or anything that is your neighbor's.

—Exod. 20:1–4, 7–8, 12–17

The people realized they did not want God speaking directly to them, so they said to Moses, "You speak for us . . . but do not let God speak to us, lest we die" (Exod. 20:19). Moses told the people not to fear, but to know that God was testing them. Then God continued to give Israel more instructions. He gave them 613 commands to help them walk as a holy nation before God. Following these commands would not make Israel righteous but would teach the people how to live as God's special nation. But even in the commands, God revealed that the only way to approach Him was through a blood sacrifice. A blood sacrifice was needed to cover sin, serve God, or even praise Him.

Questions:

❝ Were the Ten Commandments given for all people or just for Israel?
  ◆ *Just for Israel.*

❝ What is God's covenant promise to Israel?
  ◆ *That they would become a kingdom of priests and a holy nation.*

❝ What was necessary to approach God?
  ◆ *A blood sacrifice.*

19

God's Desire to Dwell with Man (the Tabernacle)

(Exodus 25–26)

After God gave Israel the commandments, He gave instructions to Moses for the nation to build a tent so God could dwell among the people as they traveled. As each person decided in their heart, they gave freely to build this tabernacle. They gave gold, silver, bronze, fine linens, animal skins, and all that was needed to make the special dwelling place for God. With their deliverance from slavery fresh in their memory, it was a joy to give to God what they had received freely because of His favor. What is amazing is that Israel gave so much that they were asked to stop giving.

Because this tabernacle would be so special, God even chose and gifted certain men with artistic skills to make each part of the tent just as God told Moses. This would be a mobile tent that they could move with them wherever God led. Wherever God's people went, the tabernacle was in the middle, and the 12 tribes camped around it, each tribe camping in the same place each time. God's design was that His presence would be in the middle of His people and that He would dwell among them. He would appear as a pillar of cloud over the tabernacle by day and a pillar of fire by night.

Each part of the tabernacle was to be built exactly as God told Moses. That was because each piece pointed to something greater. Like a shadow points to something real, the tabernacle was filled with shadows of greater things. For instance, there was only one entrance to the tabernacle, just like there is only one way into the kingdom of God. When someone entered the tabernacle, there was an altar for sacrifice, but the most important part was in the middle of the tabernacle. That special place was to be hidden behind a veil and called the Most Holy Place. Only one person, the high priest, could enter the Most Holy Place, and he could only enter once a year. Inside the Most Holy Place was the ark of the covenant. The ark was like a big wooden chest covered entirely in gold. The stones on which God wrote the Ten Commandments were kept inside the ark. The cover of the ark was special as well, with two angels facing each other with their wings stretched toward each other. The mercy seat, the area above the wings, is where God's presence would rest. As you can imagine, this place was very special. Even before the high priest entered, he offered a sacrifice to God.

You see, God always wants to dwell with His people, but just like the tabernacle, a blood sacrifice is always the first step. And just like the tent was God's temporary home, God was teaching that the temporary dwelling of the Lord is never as good as being with Him forever.

Questions:

❝ Were the tabernacle and the things in it God's focus, or did they point to something else?
  ✧ *The tabernacle and the things in it were a shadow, pointing to greater things.*

❝ Did the people give because God demanded them to give or because they wanted to give?
  ✧ *The people gave because they wanted to give.*

❝ What is the name of the room where the ark of the covenant was placed?
  ✧ *It was called the Most Holy Place.*

20

Joshua and the Spies

(Numbers 13–14)

God's people finally reached the land of Canaan, the land that God promised Abraham so long ago. God told Moses to select a man from each tribe to spy out the land He was going to give them. Moses said to the spies:

> Go . . . and see what the land is, and whether the people who dwell in it are strong or weak, whether they are few or many, and whether the land that they dwell in is good or bad. . . . Be of good courage and bring some of the fruit of the land."
>
> —Num. 13:17–20

At the end of 40 days, the 12 men came back from spying out the land God promised the nation. They reported to Moses and Aaron that it was a land flowing with milk and honey, just as God had promised. The fruit they brought back was so big that it took two men to carry it. Ten of the men continued to give their report, but it was not good. They said the people in the land were too mighty and the cities were too protected for Israel to take the land. But there were two men, Joshua and Caleb, who disagreed.

Caleb and Joshua said they could and should take the land. Even if there were giants in the land, they could overcome them with God on their side. But the people grumbled, convinced that they should elect another leader and go back to Egypt. Moses and Aaron were so sad at the people's response that they fell on their faces. Caleb and Joshua begged the people not to rebel against the Lord, but the people wanted to stone them. Finally, God declared He was going to strike all the people down, but Moses pleaded with God to pardon the people for the sake of His great name.

God did pardon the nation, but He promised that those who decided to disobey Him would not enter the land of promise. Only Caleb and Joshua would enter the land, but only after Israel wandered for 40 more years in the wilderness. That

would be enough time for everyone of that generation to die. Even though Moses told them not to, some of the people tried to enter the land anyway. But without God on their side, they lost the battle.

~ Questions: ~

❝ Was God faithful to His promise with Abraham?
  ◆ *Yes*

❝ Did Caleb and Joshua enter the land because they gave a good report or because they believed God?
  ◆ *They entered the land because they believed God.*

❝ How did God discipline the nation but still show His love for them?
  ◆ *Israel would have to wander for 40 years before entering the land of promise.*

21

Jericho: Part 1

(Joshua 1–3)

Moses was Israel's mighty deliverer. He had a very special relationship with God. But while Israel was wandering in the wilderness, Moses disobeyed God. Because he did not honor God as holy, Moses only got to see the land of promise from Mt. Nebo before he died. God chose Joshua to replace Moses and lead Israel into the land God promised Abraham so long ago. God told Joshua that He would be with him, just like He was with Moses, and that no one would be able to stand before him all the days of his life.

Just like Moses, Joshua sent out some men to spy out the land and especially the city of Jericho. The spies were almost captured, but a woman named Rahab hid them. Rahab said the whole city was fearful because they had heard of God's great power and might. The spies promised Rahab that if she placed a scarlet cord out her window, her whole family would be saved from destruction. She did exactly what they asked and was saved. Rahab became very important not only to Israel but also to the whole world.

The spies came back and reported that the whole land feared Israel. God's people were excited to enter the land. Before their first battle, God exalted Joshua to help him lead the people. Just like Moses parted the Red Sea, Joshua parted the Jordan River so the people could enter the land. The ark of the covenant, God's presence, led the way into the land of promise.

Questions:

❝ Was Rahab an Israelite or an outsider (a Gentile)?
  ◆ *She was an outsider (a Gentile).*

❝ God loves to reveal shadows in stories. Saving Rahab is a shadow of what?
  ◆ *That God would eventually save some faithful Gentiles as promised in Genesis.*

❝ Why do you think God chose the color scarlet as the color of the cord?
  ◆ *It was a shadow of Jesus's blood that brings salvation.*

22

Jericho: Part 2

(Joshua 5–6)

Here was Israel, finally about to enter the land of promise. Before they did anything more, they marked the place where they crossed the Jordan River with stones as a memorial to God. Next, they circumcised the younger generation that was born while they were wandering in the wilderness. Then, they celebrated Passover. Circumcision marked every Jew as a member of God's special people. There was no better way for God's people to prepare for their future than to remember their past—their slavery and God's mighty deliverance.

You might think that God would give Joshua an incredible battle plan in which they tricked the people inside the city of Jericho or rushed the city with some new weapon. But that's not what God had in mind. In order for the Jewish people to know it was not their strength but God's that would take the city, the plan did not involve a battle at all. Joshua was told to have armed men and priests march around the city once a day for six days. Seven priests would blow trumpets as they carried the ark of the covenant. And the people were not to make a sound until the day God told them to.

So once a day for six days, the armed men and the priests walked around the city. While they walked around the city, the priests blew their trumpets continually.

On the seventh day, instead of marching around the city once, they marched around the city seven times. Throughout the Bible, God uses the number seven to represent completion. The seventh time, as the priests blew their trumpets, Joshua said to the people, "Shout, for the Lord has given you the city. . . . Only Rahab the prostitute and all who are with her in her house shall live, because she hid the messengers whom we sent" (Josh. 6:16–17).

When the people shouted, the mighty walls of Jericho fell down, and the Jews marched into the city and devoted everything and everyone in the city to destruction. When it was over, Joshua said, "Cursed before the Lord be the man who rises up and rebuilds this city, Jericho" (Josh. 6:26). Just like that, just by obeying the command of the Lord, Israel defeated a mighty city. And the Lord was with Joshua, and his fame spread throughout the land.

Jericho: Part 2

Questions:

❝ Did God fulfill His promise to save Rahab the Gentile?
  ◆ *Yes, God was faithful to His word.*

❝ Did Israel defeat Jericho with human strength or by trusting in God's direction?
  ◆ *They defeated Jericho simply by trusting God.*

❝ Why did God choose the seventh day to destroy Jericho?
  ◆ *Seven is God's number for completion.*

23

Samson

(Judges 15–16)

The Jews conquered much of the promised land under Joshua's command. But when Joshua died, the people began to stray from God's Torah (instructions). As they followed other gods, they fell under the rule of their enemies, just as God said they would. When they cried out to God and turned from their sinful ways, God would raise up a judge. Judges were men or women God would appoint to deliver and govern Israel. But like stubborn children, Israel fell into a cycle of worshiping false gods (idolatry), enslavement by their enemies, crying out to God, God sending a judge to deliver them, worshiping God, and then starting the cycle all over again. Over and over, everyone did what they thought was right in their own eyes.

One judge was named Samson. An angel appeared to a barren woman and told her that she would have a special son. He was to be a Nazarite, which meant he would be totally devoted to God, he could never cut his hair, he could never touch a dead body, and he could never drink strong drink. Samson's parents had great belief and listened to the angel. As Samson grew, he became incredibly strong. And even though he was one of God's appointed judges, he also did what he thought was right in his own eyes. But as always, Samson's poor decisions were never outside of God's perfect plan.

Samson once killed 1,000 of God's enemies, the Philistines, with the jawbone of a donkey. Another time, he tore a lion apart with his bare hands. He was a mighty man, and his fame spread throughout the land. Samson's problem was not Israel's enemies but rather that he went his own way. Instead of marrying another Israelite, Samson fell in love with a foreign woman named Delilah. The Philistines used Delilah to trick Samson into telling her the source of his great strength.

Delilah was promised 1,100 silver coins if she could get Samson to tell her why he was so strong. The first time she asked, Samson lied to her. When she tried what he told her, it didn't work. As always, with the Spirit of God, Samson rose up and defeated the Philistines when Delilah cried out, "The Philistines are upon you, Samson!" (Judg. 16:9). But she didn't give up. She asked him again and again. He lied by saying that he had to be tied with new ropes. While he slept, she tried it, and once again, he rose up and defeated the Philistines. But she didn't give up. Delilah finally wore him down, and he told her the truth, that if his hair was cut, he would lose his strength. She cut his hair, and he was easily defeated. The Philistines poked out his eyes and put him in chains.

But as time passed, Samson's hair began to grow back. One day, the Philistines took him to their temple to mock him. While he was there, he prayed to God to avenge the Philistines for the loss of his eyes. Samson grasped the two pillars on which the temple rested, and with the Spirit of God strengthening him, he pushed the pillars apart, and the temple fell down. Samson died with the Philistines, but in his death, he killed more of God's enemies than he had in his life.

Questions:

❝ Why didn't the Jews conquer all the inhabitants of the land of Canaan?
  ◆ *Because they kept turning to idols.*

❝ Whom did God raise up to deliver Israel when their enemies enslaved them?
  ◆ *God raised up judges.*

❝ How did Samson finally lose his strength?
  ◆ *Delilah cut his hair.*

❝ Did Samson's disobedience keep God from doing what He planned?
  ◆ *No, Samson judged Israel and killed God's enemies just as God planned.*

24

David Anointed King

(1 Samuel 8–16)

One of Israel's mightiest prophets was Samuel. He was born to a woman named Hannah who was barren but cried out to God in prayer for a child. God answered Hannah's prayer. As Samuel grew older, the people started asking for a king like the other nations around them. Samuel warned them that having an earthly king would not turn out well for them, but they did not care. So God chose a king for them just like they asked. God chose Saul of the tribe of Benjamin. He was exactly what the people wanted in an earthly king. He was handsome and a head taller than everyone around him.

For a while, Saul was a good king, but it was not long before Saul chose his own way instead of following God's ways. The king's job was not to sacrifice to the Lord because God gave that job to the priests. But before a battle, instead of waiting for Samuel, Saul sacrificed to God. When Samuel arrived, he told King Saul that because he did not keep the command of the Lord, his kingdom would not continue. God then sought out a man after His own heart, and sent Samuel to anoint him as king.

God sent Samuel to Bethlehem, to a man named Jesse of the tribe of Judah. God told Samuel that the new king would be from among Jesse's sons. When Samuel saw Jesse's oldest son, he thought that surely he was the one God had chosen. But God told Samuel that it is not the outside that counts, but the inside. Jesse brought seven of his sons before Samuel, but none of them was God's chosen king. Samuel asked Jesse, "Are all your sons here?" (1 Sam. 16:11). Jesse told him the youngest son was out watching the sheep. The youngest was David. He was ruddy and handsome. God said, "Arise and anoint him, for this is he" (1 Sam. 16:12). So Samuel took a horn of oil and anointed David. "And The Spirit of God rushed upon David from that day forward" (1 Sam. 16:13). Although David was Israel's second king, he was its greatest king. And there would be another king who would come from David's heritage, and He would be the King of all Kings.

Questions:

❝ Who was Israel's first king?
- ✧ *Saul of the tribe of Benjamin.*

❝ Why did God take the kingdom away from Saul?
- ✧ *Saul chose his own way and offered a sacrifice to God instead of waiting for Samuel.*

❝ What is more important to God, the outside of a person or the inside?
- ✧ *God cares about what is in the heart.*

❝ What tribe was David from?
- ✧ *David was from the tribe of Judah.*

25

David and Goliath

(1 Samuel 17)

Even though David was chosen as the next king, he didn't become king right away. In fact, he was anointed three times before he actually became king. But after he was anointed the first time, God gave a glimpse of the heart David had for God's glory. God and Israel's enemy, the Philistines, gathered their armies for war. Saul was still the king of Israel, and his army was on one side of a hill, and the Philistines were on another hill with a valley between them. But it wasn't the Philistine's army that caused fear. It was a mighty warrior named Goliath.

Goliath was from Gad. He was almost 10 feet tall. His armor weighed more than 100 pounds, and he had been a warrior since he was a boy. With no fear, Goliath challenged anyone in Israel to fight him. He said if that person killed him, the Philistines would be their servants. But if Goliath won, the Jews would become the Philistines' servants. Goliath yelled in defiance of the armies of Israel, daring them to send a man to fight him.

David's three oldest brothers had followed King Saul to war, but David was tending his father's sheep. For 40 days, Goliath came out and challenged Israel. No Israelite came forward. One day, as David was going to check on his brothers, Goliath came out and challenged Israel again, and David heard him. David asked the men around him what the king would do for the man who killed Goliath. His brothers heard him and became angry, but David did not stop asking.

When Saul heard this, he called for David and told him that because he was only a boy, there was no way he could beat a mighty soldier like Goliath. David told Saul how he had killed both a lion and a bear while protecting his father's sheep. David said that the uncircumcised dog, Goliath, would be just like one of them because he defied the armies of the living God. Saul told David to go then, and even tried to give David his armor. But David would not go into battle with Saul's armor. Instead, he took with him five smooth stones and his sling and went to meet Goliath.

Goliath was furious when he saw young David coming toward him. Goliath told him he would feed his flesh to the birds. David simply said, "You come to me with a sword and with a spear and with a javelin, but I come to you in the name of the LORD of hosts, the God of the armies of Israel, whom you have defied . . . that all the earth may know that there is a God in Israel" (1 Sam. 17:45–46). Goliath quickly came toward David. Pulling one stone from his bag, David used his sling and struck Goliath in the forehead. Just like that, the battle was over, and Goliath fell dead, face first. David then took Goliath's sword and cut off his head. When the Philistine's saw their champion dead, they ran. But the Israelites chased them and defeated them that day.

Questions:

❝ Did David become king right away, or did he have to wait?
  ◇ *David had to wait.*

❝ Goliath is a shadow of sin and death. Was it easy or hard for David to defeat him?
  ◇ *It was easy.*

❝ Goliath had a sword and a spear. What did David have?
  ◇ *David had a sling, five stones, and the power of the Lord.*

26

Solomon Builds God's Temple

(1 Chronicles 22, 28; 2 Chronicles 1–7; 1 Kings 6)

It had been 480 years since the Israelites left Egypt. Now, they were finally going to build God's temple where His presence would dwell. King David wanted to build God's temple, but since he was a man of war, God told him that his son Solomon would be the one to build it. As a man after God's own heart, David planned ahead, gathered everything Solomon would need, and assigned all the jobs the priests would do. David also told Solomon to gain understanding in order to lead God's people. So when God asked Solomon what his heart desired, Solomon didn't choose riches or the destruction of God's enemies. Instead, he asked God for wisdom. God not only made Solomon the wisest person who ever lived but also gave him great riches.

But the most important thing to think about is that God, who is everywhere and cannot be contained, was coming to live in something made by human hands. All the plans to build the temple, which were patterned after the tabernacle God had Moses build, were given by God. Inside the temple would be the Most Holy Place where the ark of the covenant would be placed, and God's presence would rest on the mercy seat. That is the place where once a year, on the Day of Atonement, the high priest would come and sprinkle blood to cover the sins of Israel. This temple was to be spectacular, not just because of all the gold and precious materials, but because God would dwell there among His people.

King Solomon had more than 150,000 people working on the temple, which took more than seven years to build. Every stone used was prepared in the quarry where the stones came from. So when the temple was put together, no tools were used. When the temple was finally complete, Solomon dedicated it with a prayer, sacrificed 142,000 animals, and celebrated for seven days. It was truly an amazing building. God told Solomon that if he would walk in His ways, He would continue to dwell with His people. Unfortunately, Solomon married foreign women who turned his heart from following God completely. So instead of God dwelling among His people and Solomon's kingdom being established for generations, God divided the kingdom after Solomon died.

Solomon Builds God's Temple

❝ Questions: ❞

❝ How long after being delivered from Egypt was God's temple built?
  ◆ *480 years*

❝ Did Solomon have to gather all the gold, silver, and precious materials to build the temple?
  ◆ *No, his father, King David, planned ahead and gathered much of the materials.*

❝ What is the Most Holy Place, what was kept there, and how often did someone go inside?
  ◆ *It was the place where God's presence rested, on the mercy seat on the ark of the covenant. The high priest entered once a year on the Day of Atonement.*

27

Ecclesiastes: The Futility of Life

(Ecclesiastes 1–12)

Vanity, vanity, all is vanity. These are words from the wisest man who ever lived—Solomon. God asked King Solomon what he desired most, and instead of great wealth or power, he asked for wisdom. God granted his request, and Solomon lived as the wisest and the wealthiest man. Although Solomon's heart was led astray by foreign women, he used his wisdom and wealth to explore all the world had to offer. He recorded what he discovered in a book called Ecclesiastes, which means "the teacher."

Over and over in every area of life, Solomon discovered how futile or pointless life is. "All streams run to the sea, but the sea is not full," and "the eye is not satisfied with seeing, nor the ear filled with hearing" (Eccles. 1:7, 8). These phrases are samples of how he tells us that living is vanity. You can choose to live as a fool or as a wise person, and no matter what, they both die and end up in the ground. Life is vanity.

In studying the righteous man and the evil man, Solomon saw the wicked prosper and the righteous perish. That left him realizing that he could not understand God's ways. The best a man can do is to "eat and drink and be joyful" (Eccles. 8:15). Death will come to all people, and the battle does not go to the strong or the race to the fastest, but chance comes to them all. Over and over with God-given wisdom and God-given wealth, King Solomon tried to figure out life, and he summed it up as "Vanity of vanities! All is vanity" (Eccles. 1:1).

Solomon was the wisest man who ever lived. He had everything we often believe will make us happy—wealth, fame, and fortune. But in the end, he makes this statement: "The end of the matter; all has been heard. Fear God and keep his commandments, for this is the whole duty of man" (Eccles. 12:13).

Ecclesiastes: The Futility of Life

Questions:

❝ What phrase describes what King Solomon discovered about life?
- *Vanity of vanities! All is vanity.*

❝ In the end, what is the best a person can do with this life?
- *Fear God and keep His commandments.*

❝ If we know we can't really keep God's commandments, how can we do this?
- *Fear God and believe in His Son, who kept all the commandments for us.*

28

The Division of the Kingdom

(1 Kings 12–15; 2 Chronicles 10–13)

Sadly, King Solomon led Israel into idolatry. As a consequence, after Solomon's death, God divided the kingdom in two: the Northern Kingdom (Israel) and the Southern Kingdom (Judah). The Southern Kingdom was represented by the tribes of Judah and Benjamin. Benjamin was the only tribe that stayed faithful to King David's family line of Judah.

The division came about through Rehoboam's bad decision. Rehoboam was Solomon's son, and as Israel's new king, he gathered the old men for counsel. They told him to remove the heavy tax burden Solomon had on the people. They told him that if he would be a servant to the people, they would be his servants forever. But Rehoboam abandoned the counsel of the old men and gathered the young men and asked for their counsel. The young men said the exact opposite of the older men, saying he should increase the burden on the people.

The king did not listen to the wiser older men, and ten of the tribes rose up against Rehoboam. They chose Jeroboam from the tribe of Ephraim as their king and became known as Israel, or the Northern Kingdom. Israel's capital became Samaria, and Judah's capital remained Jerusalem.

Because God had appointed feasts, which required the Israelites to travel to Jerusalem, Jeroboam became worried that his people would turn back to God. So Jeroboam placed idols in two cities in the Northern Kingdom and proclaimed to Israel, "Behold your gods, O Israel, who brought you up out of the land of Egypt" (1 Kings 12:28). So Israel began to worship idols, and none of the kings after Jeroboam did what was pleasing in God's eyes. They fell further and further into idolatry. But all the kings in Judah were from the line of David. Some were good, and others were not, but because of God's great love for His people, He sent prophets again and again to warn them of the consequences of following their own ways rather than His.

The Division of the Kingdom

Questions:

❝ Why did God divide the kingdom in two?
 ✧ *Because King Solomon fell into idolatry.*

❝ What do we call the two kingdoms?
 ✧ *We call the Southern Kingdom, Judah and the Northern Kingdom, Israel.*

❝ Which kingdom always had a descendant of David on the throne?
 ✧ *Judah*

29

Elijah on Mount Carmel

(1 Kings 18:16–40)

In the Northern Kingdom, one of Israel's kings—Ahab—was far worse than any other. King Ahab led the people of Israel to worship false gods. This grieved the prophet Elijah. So Elijah told King Ahab to assemble all the people of Israel at Mount Carmel, including the 450 prophets of Baal, who was a false god. When all the people arrived, Elijah said to them, "If the LORD is God, follow him; but if Baal, then follow him" (1 Kings 18:21). The people said nothing.

> Then Elijah said to the people, "I, even I only, am left a prophet of the LORD, but Baal's prophets are 450 men. Let two bulls be given to us, and let them choose one bull for themselves and cut it in pieces and lay it on the wood, but put no fire to it. And I will prepare the other bull and lay it on the wood and put no fire to it. And you call upon the name of your god, and I will call upon the name of the LORD, and the God who answers by fire, he is God." And all the people answered, "It is well spoken."
>
> —1 Kings 18:22–24

The prophets of Baal prepared their sacrifice, and then they called on the name of Baal from morning until noon. But there was no response; no one answered. And they danced around the altar they had made.

At noon, Elijah began to make fun of them. "Cry aloud, for he is a god. Either he is musing, or he is relieving himself, or he is on a journey, or perhaps he is asleep and must be awakened" (1 Kings 18:27). They shouted louder and cut themselves with swords until they bled. But there was no response; no one answered.

Then, Elijah repaired the altar of the Lord, which was in ruins, and dug a trench around it. Then he told the people to pour four buckets of water on the wood. They did that several times until the trench was full of water.

Then, Elijah stepped forward and prayed:

> O Lord, God of Abraham, Isaac, and Israel, let it be known this day that you are God in Israel, and that I am your servant, and that I have done all

these things at your word. Answer me, O LORD, that this people may know that you, O LORD, are God, and that you have turned their hearts back.

—1 Kings 18:36–37

Then the fire of the Lord fell and burned up the sacrifice, the wood, the stones, and the soil. It also licked up the water in the trench. When all the people saw this, they fell down and cried, "The LORD he is God; the LORD he is God" (1 Kings 18:39).

Then Elijah commanded them to kill all the prophets of Baal. And so they did.

Questions:

❝ Who was the worst King of Israel, and what did he do?
 ◆ *King Ahab led Israel to serve false gods.*

❝ What challenge did Elijah present to the prophets of Baal?
 ◆ *To call upon their false god to burn a sacrifice.*

❝ When God won the challenge, what did the people do?
 ◆ *They fell down and cried, "The Lord he is God."*

30

Jonah

(Jonah 1–4)

Jonah was a prophet sent by God. He wasn't sent to Israel but to the Gentiles. Jonah was sent to Nineveh, the capital of Assyria. The Assyrians were one of the most ruthless conquering nations in history. Jonah was sent to warn Nineveh that God was going to judge them because of their evil ways. Jonah knew God would be gracious and forgive them if they repented, so rather than warn Nineveh, Jonah went in the opposite direction by getting on a ship headed to Tarshish.

However, trying to flee from God's plan did not turn out well for Jonah. God sent a great storm that threatened to sink the ship he was on. In fear, the sailors cried out to their gods. Jonah was sleeping below deck. The sailors woke up Jonah and casts lots to see who was responsible for the storm. Casting lots was an ancient way of finding out what a god thought about a situation. The lot fell on Jonah, and the sailors remembered that Jonah said he was running from God. Wanting the storm to end, they asked Jonah what they needed to do. Jonah told them to throw him overboard and God would end the storm. They didn't want to, and they even cried out to the Lord to not let them die because of Jonah. But the storm continued, so they tossed Jonah overboard. Immediately, the storm stopped. Amazingly, the men offered a sacrifice to the Lord.

There Jonah was, in the water, without any way to run from God. So God sent a great fish to swallow Jonah, and he spent three days and three nights in the belly of the fish. Finally, remembering that salvation belongs to the Lord, Jonah cried out to God in prayer. And God, being gracious, spoke to the fish, and it spit Jonah out on dry land.

God spoke to Jonah again about going to Nineveh. This time, Jonah listened. He went to Nineveh and told them that in 40 days, God would judge them because of their wickedness. Just like Jonah thought, all the people believed and turned from their wickedness in hope that God would not destroy them. And sure enough, just like Jonah thought, God noticed how they humbled themselves and then revealed His great mercy to them.

Sadly, Jonah pouted and became angry because God was gracious. God asked Jonah why He shouldn't pity so many people made in his image and even pity the cattle He created. And with that, the story of Jonah ends.

Jonah

Questions:

❝ Did God send Jonah to his chosen people Israel or to the Gentiles, people who did not know him?
  ◇ *God sent Jonah to the Gentiles.*

❝ When Jonah tried to run from God, what did God do?
  ◇ *He sent a fish to swallow him, causing him to cry out in prayer.*

❝ God shows great love for all people, but what does He reveal in mentioning cattle?
  ◇ *His great love includes all His creation.*

31

Exile of Israel and Judah

(1 Chronicles 5; 2 Kings 17; 2 Chronicles 22; Deuteronomy 28:62–65; 2 Kings 24)

Israel had 20 kings over a couple hundred years, and none of them did what was pleasing in God's eyes. God sent prophets like Elijah, Elisha, and Hosea to call the people back to Him. But they still set up for themselves sacred pillars and wooden images on every hill and under every green tree. God intended to drive out the nations that were in the land of promise because of their idolatry, but just like them, Israel provoked the Lord to anger and served idols. Israel did not listen to the prophets God sent and did not keep His commandments. So God stirred up a foreign king to conquer them. First, the Assyrians conquered the Reubenites, the Gadites, and the half tribe of Manasseh. Then 20 years later, they conquered the capital of Samaria. Israel battled for three years, but without God's protection, they were conquered and scattered just as God had warned.

Unlike Israel, Judah had a mix of bad and good kings. But much like Israel, Judah had a problem with idolatry. Even though Jerusalem was the capital where the temple was located, the kings allowed high places for idol worship there. Kings Abijah, Ahaz, Manasseh, and Zedekiah were wicked and led Judah further into idolatry. Kings Asa, Uzziah, and Hezekiah followed the Lord. But even with the temple, the fall of Israel, and the warnings of God's prophets, Judah did not return to God.

The Babylonian King Nebuchadnezzar invaded Judah and destroyed the temple Solomon had built for God's presence. As was the custom of Babylonian kings, Nebuchadnezzar carried many of the people far away from their land. The prophets Isaiah, Habakkuk, and Zephaniah told of the coming destruction God was sending to Judah.

But to understand the Babylonian captivity, we must know that not only was the exile prophesied, but a return to the land was also prophesied. Others may dwell in the land, but God gave it as a possession for His chosen people. Yes, their disobedience caused them to be removed from the land. But yes, God's faithfulness to His word meant He would fulfill His promise to Abraham, and they would return.

Questions:

❝ Who went into exile first for their idolatry Israel or Judah?
  ◆ *Israel. They were conquered by the Assyrians.*

❝ Who conquered the Southern Kingdom (Judah)?
  ◆ *The Babylonians*

❝ Although God scattered the entire nation of Israel for their idolatry, was the exile permanent?
  ◆ *No. He prophesied their return to the land.*

32

Daniel and the Lions' Den

(Daniel 6)

Because of the Israelites' idolatry, they were removed from the land of promise. When the Babylonians conquered the Southern Kingdom (Judah), many of the Israelites were carried away. But later, even when the Persians conquered the Babylonians, nothing changed for God's people. Now Daniel was from the tribe of Judah, and God had given him wisdom and favor. Darius, the King of Persia, appointed Daniel as one of the three high officials over the entire kingdom. The spirit in Daniel was so great that the king was going to put him over the whole kingdom, but that stirred up jealousy in all the other officials.

The other officials could not find fault with Daniel, but they did want to destroy him. So they decided to pit Daniel's God against Darius. They knew Daniel prayed to God three times a day, so they tricked the king into making a law he could not change. For the next 30 days, anyone who prayed to anyone other than Darius would be thrown into a lions' den.

When Daniel knew the king had signed the new law, he went to his house where he prayed three times a day and gave thanks to God as he had always done. The officials quickly ran to the king and told him that Daniel was praying to God. Even though the jealous officials did their best to tell the king that Daniel had no regard for him, the king was sad and looked for a way to save Daniel. But when the officials reminded Darius that the law could not be changed, he had no choice but to throw Daniel into a den of lions.

As the king had Daniel thrown into the lions' den, he said, "May your God whom you serve continually deliver you!" (Daniel 6:16). Darius tossed and turned all night hoping Daniel would survive. At the break of day, he ran to the lions' den and cried out, "O Daniel, servant of the living God, has your God, whom you serve continually, been able to deliver you from the lions?" (Dan. 6:20). Daniel said that God sent an angel to shut the mouths of the lions. The king was so happy. In fact, he was so happy that he threw the jealous officials into the lions' den. Then king Darius made a decree to the whole nation saying that "people are to tremble and fear the God of Daniel. . . . He delivers and rescues" (Dan. 6:26, 27).

Daniel and the Lions' Den

Questions:

❝ What was the reason the other officials did not like Daniel?
- *They were jealous of him.*

❝ What did Daniel do when Darius made the law he could not pray to God?
- *He went to his house and prayed.*

❝ How did Darius react to God saving Daniel from the lions?
- *He made a decree that everyone should tremble and fear God.*

33

Hananiah, Mishael, and Azariah

(Daniel 3)

According to the Bible, God is the one who raises up kings and lowers them. But King Nebuchadnezzar thought it was his own might that allowed him to conquer nations. So when God used King Nebuchadnezzar to conquer and remove Judah from the land because of their idolatry, the king built a great statue of himself for everyone to worship. With all the officials gathered to dedicate the statue, it was proclaimed that when the horn sounded, everyone must fall down and worship the image or be thrown into a fiery furnace.

Now there were three Israelites who had great favor with the king and were placed over the affairs of Babylon. Their Hebrew names were Hananiah, Mishael, and Azariah, but the king called them by their Babylonian names—Shadrach, Meshach, and Abednego. These three men did not bow down to worship the idol, because even though they were in exile, they still served God. So when a certain man created trouble by telling Nebuchadnezzar that Shadrach, Meschach, and Abednego refused to worship his idol, the king became extremely angry.

When they were brought before Nebuchadnezzar, he asked if it was true that they would not worship the Babylonian gods or the golden image he made. Before letting them answer, he gave them the opportunity to hear the horns, bow down, and worship as his law demanded. But immediately they gave King Nebuchadnezzar his answer.

Shadrach, Meshach, and Abednego said, "Our God whom we serve is able to deliver us from the burning fiery furnace, and he will deliver us out of your hand, O king. But if not, be it known to you, O king, that we will not serve your gods or worship the golden image that you have set up" (Dan. 3:17–18). Nebuchadnezzar was filled with fury and had the fire heated seven times hotter than usual. In fact, the fire was so hot that the flames killed the men whose job it was to throw them into the fire.

The king arose quickly and asked, "Did we not cast three men bound into the fire? . . . . But I see four men unbound, walking in the midst of the fire, and they are not hurt; and the appearance of the fourth is like a son of the gods" (Dan. 3:24–25). Seeing this, the king ran to the door and said, "Shadrach, Meshach, and Abednego, servants of the Most High God, come out, and come here!" (Dan. 3:26). With all the officials, governors, and counselors gathered, all three of the Hebrews walked out. Everyone saw that not only were they still alive but the fire did not harm them in any way. In fact, their clothes did not even smell like smoke.

Nebuchadnezzar said, "Blessed be the God of Shadrach, Meshach, and Abednego, who sent his angel and delivered his servants, who trusted in him, and set aside the king's command, and yielded up their bodies rather than serve and worship any god except their own God" (Dan. 3:28). He then confessed that no other god could have delivered them in this way and decreed that no one was to ever speak against God or they would be torn apart. Finally, the king restored and promoted them. Just like that, God gave His people the freedom to worship him in a foreign land.

Questions:

❝ What were Shadrach, Meshach, and Abednego's Hebrew names?
- *Hananiah, Mishael, and Azariah*

❝ What did they say about God and His ability to deliver them?
- *He can deliver us, He will deliver us, but even if He doesn't, we will not bow down.*

❝ What does their statement say about how all believers should serve God?
- *We should always pray knowing that God can and will answer. But even if He doesn't, we should remain faithful.*

34

Prophecy of the Coming King (Book of Isaiah)

(Isaiah summary)

One of the most powerful books of the Bible is the Old Testament book of Isaiah. Isaiah was a prophet during the time the kingdom was divided, and he prophesied to Judah for about 50 years. King Solomon's sin led to the division of Israel into the Northern Kingdom and the Southern Kingdom. Each kingdom did not listen to God's prophets who called them to return to Him and warned them of their exile from the promised land. The Northern Kingdom had already been exiled when the Assyrians conquered them. And the Southern Kingdom was stuck in the middle of incredible idolatry and evil. Isaiah prophesied during the reign of Kings Uzziah, Jotham, Ahaz, and Hezekiah. He warned of the judgment that was coming to the Southern Kingdom of Judah because they would not stop their great sinfulness and idolatry.

But more than any other Old Testament book, Isaiah speaks of the Messiah who would one day save Israel and bring peace and safety. Isaiah said the Messiah would be a light to all nations. But the most beautiful part of Isaiah is the prophecy of the Messiah who would save His people, not with a mighty army but as a suffering servant. Here are the first nine verses of Isaiah 53:

> Who has believed what he has heard from us?
>   And to whom has the arm of the Lord been revealed?
> For he grew up before him like a young plant,
>   and like a root out of dry ground;
> he had no form or majesty that we should look at him,
>   and no beauty that we should desire him.
> He was despised and rejected by men,
>   a man of sorrows and acquainted with grief;
> and as one from whom men hide their faces
>   he was despised, and we esteemed him not.
> Surely he has borne our griefs
>   and carried our sorrows;
> yet we esteemed him stricken,
>   smitten by God, and afflicted.
> But he was pierced for our transgressions;
>   he was crushed for our iniquities;
> upon him was the chastisement that brought us peace,
>   and with his wounds we are healed.
> All we like sheep have gone astray;
>   we have turned—every one—to his own way;
> and the Lord has laid on him
>   the iniquity of us all.
> He was oppressed, and he was afflicted,
>   yet he opened not his mouth;
> like a lamb that is led to the slaughter,
>   and like a sheep that before its shearers is silent,
>   so he opened not his mouth.
> By oppression and judgment he was taken away;

Prophecy of the Coming King (Book of Isaiah)

>   and as for his generation, who considered
>   that he was cut off out of the land of the living,
>   stricken for the transgression of my people?
>   And they made his grave with the wicked
>   and with a rich man in his death,
>   although he had done no violence,
>   and there was no deceit in his mouth.

Isaiah is full of warnings to Judah that they should return to the Lord. Over and over, God's warnings reveal His great mercy and faithfulness to His covenant with Abraham, Isaac, and Jacob. But Isaiah is also full of Messianic prophesies that point to aspects of the Messiah's coming, that He will be born of a virgin, that God's Spirit will rest on Him, and that He will be called Immanuel—God with us.

Questions:

❝ Did Isaiah prophesy to the Northern Kingdom or the Southern Kingdom?
  ◇ *The Southern Kingdom*

❝ Of whom does Isaiah speak more than any other book in the Old Testament?
  ◇ *Isaiah speaks of the Messiah.*

❝ Isaiah says the Messiah would be called Immanuel. What does the name Immanuel mean?
  ◇ *God with us*

Bible Sound Off (Catechism)

Introductory (Ages 2–8)

1. Who made you?
   God

2. What else did God make?
   God made all things.

3. Why did God make all things?
   For His own glory.

4. Why do things work as they do?
   God has so decreed it.

5. How do we learn about God?
   God reveals Himself.

6. Where does God reveal Himself?
   In His word, nature, dreams, and visions.

7. What does God reveal in nature?
   His character, law, and wrath.

8. What more is revealed in His word?
   God's mercy toward His people.

9. Where is God's word found?
   The Bible is God's word.

10. How many Gods are there?
   God is one: God the Father—God the Son—God the Holy Spirit.

Introductory (Ages 2–8)

11. Where is God?
 He is everywhere.

12. How long has God existed?
 He has always been.

13. Who is God?
 God is the first and best of all beings.

14. What is God like?
 God is a spirit, is eternal, and is a personal being. He is perfect in holiness and is all-powerful and all-knowing.

15. How does God relate to creation?
 God is the creator, redeemer, preserver, and ruler of the universe.

16. How is man unique?
 He bears God's image.

17. Who was the first man?
 Adam

18. What was Adam like at creation?
 He was good.

19. Did Adam remain good?
 No, he sinned.

20. What is sin?
 Any thought or deed that doesn't bring God glory.

21. What does it mean to give glory?
 To show honor and enjoy God as the greatest.

❝ **22. What is the penalty for sin?**
 ◇ *Death.*

❝ **23. What did Adam's sin bring?**
 ◇ *Death came to all men.*

❝ **24. How did Adam's sin affect men?**
 ◇ *We all sinned in Adam.*

❝ **25. Must all men die for their sins?**
 ◇ *No, God elected some to life.*

❝ **26. How may we be saved from sin and death?**
 ◇ *Only through faith in Jesus Christ.*

❝ **27. Who is Jesus Christ?**
 ◇ *The eternal Son of God.*

❝ **28. Did Jesus ever sin?**
 ◇ *No, only He is righteous.*

❝ **29. What did Jesus do for His people?**
 ◇ *He conquered sin and death.*

❝ **30. How did He conquer sin and death?**
 ◇ *He absorbed God's wrath for sin by dying, then rose again.*

❝ **31. What else did Christ conquer?**
 ◇ *All his enemies.*

❝ **32. Are His enemies powerful?**
 ◇ *They have come to nothing.*

❝ **33. What did Jesus give to His people?**
 ◇ *His own righteousness.*

Introductory (Ages 2–8)

66. 34. What did Jesus take from His people?
◇ All their sin.

66. 35. How is Christ's work brought to His people?
◇ By the Holy Spirit.

66. 36. What does the Holy Spirit do?
◇ He gives life through faith.

66. 37. What is faith?
◇ Complete trust in what God says because of who He is.

66. 38. How do we recognize true faith?
◇ It yields good works.

66. 39. Who are God's children?
◇ Those who love and trust Jesus.

66. 40. What are all God's children called when they gather?
◇ His church.

66. 41. What are the traits of His church?
◇ Love for one another.

66. 42. Who is head of the church?
◇ Jesus Christ.

66. 43. Is His church perfect?
◇ No, it is being perfected.

66. 44. When will it be perfect?
◇ After Christ's return.

66. 45. What happens to the earth when Christ returns?
◇ God creates a new heaven and earth.

❝ **46. What happens to men when Christ returns?**
◇ *Christ judges all men's deeds.*

❝ **47. What happens to those Christ judges?**
◇ *The righteous dwell with Him forever, and the guilty perish apart from Him forever.*

❝ **48. What is the bad news for all men?**
◇ *All have sinned, and all stand condemned.*

❝ **49. What is the good news?**
◇ *In mercy, God made a way to save sinners through Jesus's life, death, and resurrection.*

❝ **50. How do we know we are God's children?**
◇ *The Spirit of God bears witness with our spirit that we are children of God.*

❝ **Bonus – What is the good news?**
◇ *In mercy, God made a way to save sinners through Jesus's life, death, and resurrection.*

❝ **(Long Version)**
◇ *There is one God who made everything seen and unseen. He made man in His image. He made him good, but man sinned. God would be just if He punished man forever for his sin, but in His infinite mercy, God made a way to save man. He sent Jesus, the eternal Son of God, fully God and fully man, to live a life we should have lived. Jesus suffered and died a death we deserved, but by the power of the Spirit, He was raised from the dead. He ascended to heaven, and for those who will believe in Him, He will give them the new birth and will give them the Spirit to live in them. One day, Christ will return, judge all men's deeds, and dwell forever with all those who believed.*

Intermediate (Ages 6–12)

1. Who made you?
 ⬥ God.

2. What else did God make?
 ⬥ God made all things.

3. Why did God make all things?
 ⬥ For His own glory.

4. Why do things work as they do?
 ⬥ God has so decreed it.

5. How do we learn about God?
 ⬥ God reveals Himself.

6. Where does God reveal Himself?
 ⬥ In His word, nature, dreams, and visions.

7. What does God reveal in nature?
 ⬥ His character, law, and wrath.

8. What more is revealed in His word?
 ⬥ God's mercy toward His people.

9. Where is God's word found?
 ⬥ The Bible is God's word.

10. How many Gods are there?
 ⬥ God is one: God the Father, God the Son, God the Holy Spirit.

11. Where is God?
- He is everywhere.

12. How long has God existed?
- He has always been.

13. Who is God?
- God is the first and best of all beings.

14. What is God like?
- God is a spirit, is eternal, and is a personal being. He is perfect in holiness and is all-powerful and all-knowing.

15. How does God relate to creation?
- God is the creator, redeemer, preserver, and ruler of the universe.

16. Who wrote the Bible?
- Obedient men who were led by God the Holy Spirit.

17. What does it mean to give glory?
- To show honor and enjoy God as the greatest.

18. Why should you glorify God?
- Because He alone deserves glory.

19. Can you see God?
- No, I cannot see God, but He always sees me.

20. Does God know all things?
- Yes, nothing can be hidden from God.

21. Can God do all things?
- Yes, God is in heaven and does as He pleases.

Intermediate (Ages 6–12)

22. What does it mean that God is sovereign?
   God has the right, power, and authority to govern all things.

23. What does it mean that God is holy?
   God is set apart from all other beings. He is perfect and pure.

24. What does it mean that God is just?
   God always does what is right.

25. Where do you learn how to love and obey God?
   In the Bible alone through His Spirit.

26. What did God use to create everything?
   God created everything out of nothing.

27. How is man unique?
   He bears God's image.

28. Who was the first man?
   Adam.

29. Who were our first parents?
   Adam and Eve.

30. What was Adam like at creation?
   He was good.

31. Did Adam remain good?
   No, he sinned.

32. Of what were our first parents made?
   God made the body of Adam out of the ground and formed Eve from the body of Adam.

33. What did God give Adam and Eve besides bodies?
   He gave them souls that could never die.

34. What is your soul?
   The part of me that lives forever.

35. Who tempted them to sin?
   The devil deceived Eve. Adam willingly ate the fruit Eve gave him instead of obeying God.

36. What came into the world through sin?
   Death.

37. Did Adam act for himself alone?
   No, he represented all mankind.

38. What is sin?
   Any thought or deed that doesn't bring God glory.

39. What is the penalty for sin?
   Death.

40. What did Adam's sin bring?
   Death came to all men.

41. How did Adam's sin affect all men?
   We all sinned in Adam.

42. Must all men die for sin?
   No, God elected some to life.

43. How may we be saved from sin and death?
   Only through faith in Jesus Christ.

Intermediate (Ages 6–12)

44. Who is Jesus Christ?
 The eternal Son of God.

45. Did Jesus ever sin?
 No, only He is righteous.

46. What did Jesus do for His people?
 He conquered sin and death.

47. How did He conquer sin and death?
 He absorbed God's wrath for sin by dying then rising again.

48. What else did Christ conquer?
 All his enemies.

49. Are His enemies powerful?
 They have come to nothing.

50. What did He give to His people?
 His own righteousness.

51. What did He take from His people?
 All their sin.

52. How is Christ's work brought to His people?
 By the Holy Spirit.

53. What does the Holy Spirit do?
 He gives life through faith.

54. What is faith?
 Complete trust in what God says because of who He is.

55. How do we recognize true faith?
 It yields good works.

56. Who are God's children?
   ◇ *Those who love and trust Jesus.*

57. What are all God's children called when they gather?
   ◇ *The church.*

58. What are the traits of His church?
   ◇ *Love for one another.*

59. Who is head of the church?
   ◇ *Jesus Christ.*

60. Is His church perfect?
   ◇ *No, it is being perfected.*

61. When will it be perfect?
   ◇ *After Christ's return.*

62. What happens to the earth when Christ returns?
   ◇ *God creates a new heaven and earth.*

63. What happens to men when Christ returns?
   ◇ *Christ judges all men's deeds.*

64. What happens to those Christ deems righteous?
   ◇ *They dwell with Him forever.*

65. What happens to those Christ condemns?
   ◇ *They perish forever.*

66. How do we know we are God's children?
   ◇ *The Spirit of God bears witness with our spirit that we are children of God.*

67. Who can give a sinner a new heart?
   ◇ *The Holy Spirit alone.*

Intermediate (Ages 6–12)

68. What is getting this new heart called?
◇ Regeneration.

69. Can anyone earn salvation?
◇ None can earn it.

70. Why can none be saved through works?
◇ Because all have sinned and are already condemned to death.

71. Did our Lord Jesus Christ ever commit the least sin?
◇ No, he is perfectly righteous.

72. How could the Son of God suffer?
◇ Christ, the Son of God, became a man that He might obey and suffer in our nature.

73. What is meant by the atonement?
◇ Christ's satisfying divine justice in order to cover the sins of God's children.

74. What is justification?
◇ It is God's forgiving sinners and declaring them righteous in Christ.

75. What is sanctification?
◇ It is God's making sinners holy in heart and conduct like His Son.

76. For whom did Christ obey and suffer?
◇ For those whom the Father had given Him.

77. What kind of death did Christ die?
◇ The painful and shameful death of the cross.

78. Who will be saved?
◇ Only those who believe in Jesus Christ.

79. What does it mean to repent?
◇ To turn from our ways to follow God's ways.

80. What does it mean to believe or have faith in Christ?
- To trust in Christ alone for salvation.

81. Can you repent and believe in Christ by your own power?
- No, I can do nothing good without the help of God the Holy Spirit.

82. What tribe was Jesus from?
- As prophesied, the Messiah came from the tribe of Judah.

83. Who were Jesus's mother and father?
- Jesus was born to Mary and adopted as a son by her husband Joseph.

84. How many offices does Christ have?
- Christ has three offices.

85. What are they?
- The offices of prophet, priest, and king.

86. How is Christ a prophet?
- Christ proclaims to us the will of God.

87. How is Christ a priest?
- Christ died for our sins and pleads with God for us.

88. How is Christ a king?
- Christ rules over us and defends us.

89. How many commandments did God give Israel on Mount Sinai?
- 613.

90. What do we call the commandments God wrote on stone?
- The ten commandments.

91. What do the first four commandments teach?
- Our duty to God.

Intermediate (Ages 6–12)

92. What do the last six commandments teach?
◇ Our duty to our fellow men.

93. What is the sum of the ten commandments?
◇ To love God with all my heart, soul, mind, and strength, and my neighbor as myself.

94. What is the first commandment?
◇ You shall have no other gods before me.

95. What does the first commandment teach us?
◇ To worship God alone.

96. What is the second commandment?
◇ You shall not make for yourself a carved image.

97. What does the second commandment teach us?
◇ To worship God alone and flee idolatry.

98. What is the third commandment?
◇ You shall not take the name of the Lord your God in vain.

99. What does the third commandment teach us?
◇ To reverence God's name, words, and works.

100. What is the fourth commandment?
◇ Remember the Sabbath day to keep it holy.

101. What does the fourth commandment teach us?
◇ To rest and remember how God has delivered us.

102. What is the fifth commandment?
◇ Honor your father and your mother that your days may be long in the land, which the Lord God is giving you.

❝ **103. What does the fifth commandment teach us?**
◇ To embrace God's wisdom in choosing my parents and to love His ways.

❝ **104. What is the sixth commandment?**
◇ You shall not murder.

❝ **105. What does the sixth commandment teach us?**
◇ To value life and flee from angry passions.

❝ **106. What is the seventh commandment?**
◇ You shall not commit adultery.

❝ **107. What does the seventh commandment teach us?**
◇ To be pure in heart and hold fast to our spouse.

❝ **108. What is the eighth commandment?**
◇ You shall not steal.

❝ **109. What does the eighth commandment teach us?**
◇ To be honest, industrious, and respect the possessions of others.

❝ **110. What is the ninth commandment?**
◇ You shall not bear false witness against your neighbor.

❝ **111. What does the ninth commandment teach us?**
◇ To tell the truth regardless of the consequences and flee dishonest gain.

❝ **112. What is the tenth commandment?**
◇ You shall not covet.

❝ **113. What does the tenth commandment teach us?**
◇ To be content with what we have.

Intermediate (Ages 6–12)

114. Can any man keep God's commandments perfectly?
◇ Except Christ, no man since the fall of Adam ever did or can keep God's commandments perfectly.

115. Of what use are the ten commandments to us?
◇ They reveal God's ways and show our need of a Savior.

116. What is prayer?
◇ Prayer is talking to God to worship Him; express thankfulness, needs, and desires; and confess our sins.

117. In whose name should we pray?
◇ Only in the name of Christ.

118. What has Christ given us to teach us how to pray?
◇ The Lord's Prayer.

119. Repeat the Lord's Prayer.
◇ Our Father which art in heaven, Hallowed be thy name. Thy kingdom come, Thy will be done in earth, as it is in heaven. Give us this day our daily bread. And forgive us our debts, as we forgive our debtors. And lead us not into temptation, but deliver us from evil: For thine is the kingdom, and the power, and the glory, for ever. Amen (Matt. 6:9–13 KJV).

120. How many sacraments are there?
◇ Two.

121. What are they?
◇ Baptism and the Lord's Supper.

122. Who appointed these sacraments?
◇ The Lord Jesus Christ.

123. What sign is used in baptism?
- The immersion (covering) of the body in water.

124. What does baptism signify?
- That we who are cleansed from sin are dead to the world and now alive in Christ.

125. In whose name are we baptized?
- In the name of the Father, and of the Son, and of the Holy Ghost.

126. Who are to be baptized?
- Those whose faith is in Christ alone for salvation.

127. What is the Lord's Supper?
- The eating of bread and drinking of wine in remembrance of the sufferings and death of Christ.

128. What does the bread represent?
- The body of Christ, broken for our sins.

129. What does the wine represent?
- The blood of Christ, shed for our salvation.

130. Who should partake of the Lord's Supper?
- Only those who love and trust Jesus.

131. What is spiritual adoption?
- Adoption is an act of God's free grace where we become God's children and have rights to all privileges as sons and daughters of God.

132. What benefits do God's children receive?
- Assurance of God's love, peace of conscience, joy in the Holy Spirit, increasing grace, and perseverance to the end.

Intermediate (Ages 6–12)

❝ 133. What is marriage's highest purpose?
◇ To display the gospel to the world.

❝ 134. How should a husband relate to his wife?
◇ Like Christ relates to His church.

❝ 135. How does Christ relate to His church?
◇ He gave Himself up for her to make her holy.

❝ 136. How does a husband love his wife like Christ loves His church?
◇ Only by the power of the Holy Spirit.

❝ 137. How should a wife relate to her husband?
◇ She submits as unto the Lord.

❝ 138. How does a wife submit to her husband?
◇ Only by the power of the Holy Spirit.

❝ 139. Did Christ remain in the tomb after His crucifixion?
◇ No, He rose from the tomb on the third day after His death.

❝ 140. Where is Christ now?
◇ In heaven, interceding for the saints.

❝ 141. Will Christ come again?
◇ Yes, at the last day, Christ will come to judge the world.

❝ 142. What is hell?
◇ A place of dreadful and endless torment created for demons.

❝ 143. What will become of the righteous?
◇ They will live forever in the presence of God.

❝ 144. What will become of the wicked on the Day of Judgment?
◇ They shall be cast into hell.

❝ **145. What is heaven?**
◇ A glorious place where the righteous shall be forever with God and God with them.

❝ **146. What do angels do?**
◇ God created all the angels to do His will and to praise His name.

❝ **147. What is God's providence toward the angels?**
◇ God by His providence permitted some of the angels, willfully and irrecoverably, to fall into sin and damnation.

❝ **148. What are those angels called that God permitted to fall?**
◇ Demons.

❝ **149. Who was the angel that God permitted to lead other angels to damnation?**
◇ Lucifer.

❝ **150. What did God change Lucifer's name to?**
◇ Satan.

❝ **151. What do demons do today?**
◇ Demons attempt to advance the kingdom of Satan and destroy God's elect.

❝ **152. What do angels do today?**
◇ Strive to bring God glory by doing all He commands and minister to God's elect.

❝ **153. What has God decreed for Satan and his demons?**
◇ They shall be cast into hell for eternity.

❝ **154. What is the last enemy to be cast into hell?**
◇ Death.

Intermediate (Ages 6–12)

155. What shall happen to the earth?
◇ God will destroy it and make all things new.

156. What promise does God fulfill to His elect into eternity?
◇ God will be their God, and they shall be His people.

157. What is the good news?
◇ In mercy, God made a way to save sinners through Jesus's life, death, and resurrection.

(Long Version)
◇ There is one God who made everything seen and unseen. He made man in His image. He made him good, but man sinned. God would be just if He punished man forever for his sin, but in His infinite mercy, God made a way to save man. He sent Jesus, the eternal Son of God, fully God and fully man, to live a life we should have lived. Jesus suffered and died a death we deserved, but by the power of the Spirit, He was raised from the dead. He ascended to heaven, and for those who will believe in Him, He will give them the new birth and give them the Spirit to live in them. One day, Christ will return, judge all men's deeds, and dwell forever with all those who believed.

Jewish Bible Timeline (Ages 2+)

❝ 1. What person did God choose to make a blessing to all nations?
   ◇ Abraham

❝ 2. Was Abraham righteous when God called him?
   ◇ No, he worshipped idols.

❝ 3. When was Abraham declared righteous?
   ◇ When the Bible said he believed God.

❝ 4. What kind of covenant did God make with Abraham?
   ◇ An unconditional covenant.

❝ 5. What is an unconditional covenant?
   ◇ A covenant rooted in the faithfulness of God alone.

❝ 6. What did God promise Abraham in His unconditional covenant?
   ◇ God promised Abraham land, that he would have descendants, and that all the families of the earth would be blessed through him.

❝ 7. What was the name of Abraham's son conceived through the flesh?
   ◇ Ishmael, who was conceived by a slave woman.

❝ 8. What is the name of Abraham's son conceived through the promise of God?
   ◇ Isaac, who was conceived by Abraham's wife, Sarah, according to the promise of God.

❝ 9. What became of Ishmael?
   ◇ God said he would become a great nation, but his hand would be against everyone and everyone's hand against him.

Jewish Bible Timeline (Ages 2+)

❝ **10. Who was Isaac's firstborn son?**
 ◇ Esau was the Isaac's firstborn.

❝ **11. Did Esau get the firstborn blessing?**
 ◇ No, the younger son Jacob received the blessing through trickery.

❝ **12. Did Jacob need to resort to trickery to get the firstborn blessing?**
 ◇ No, God had already promised that the older son would serve the younger.

❝ **13. What did God change Jacob's name to?**
 ◇ Israel.

❝ **14. What does the name Israel mean?**
 ◇ One who wrestles with God.

❝ **15. How many sons did Jacob have?**
 ◇ He had 12 sons.

❝ **16. Which of Jacob's sons was sold into slavery by his brothers?**
 ◇ Joseph.

❝ **17. Why did Joseph's brothers sell him into slavery?**
 ◇ Jacob loved Joseph more, and it made his brothers jealous.

❝ **18. Where did Joseph end up after being sold by his brothers?**
 ◇ Joseph was enslaved in Egypt.

❝ **19. What did Joseph's brothers do to deceive their father Jacob?**
 ◇ They dipped Joseph's coat in blood and told Jacob an animal killed him.

❝ **20. What became of Joseph in Egypt?**
 ◇ God was with him, and he gained favor with the Pharaoh of Egypt.

❝ **21. How did Joseph provide food to his family during a famine?**
 ◇ Pharaoh made Joseph second in charge of all of Egypt, including selling food.

22. Did Joseph's brothers recognize him when they came to buy food?
◇ *No, but Joseph recognized them and treated them roughly before showing mercy.*

23. What became of Jacob's family when they found Joseph in Egypt?
◇ *Jacob and his family moved to Egypt.*

24. What became of God's people in Egypt?
◇ *They multiplied greatly, and Pharaoh enslaved them out of fear.*

25. Who are the 12 tribes of Israel that received a portion of the promised land?
◇ *Rueben, Simeon, Judah, Dan, Naphtali, Gad, Asher, Issachar, Zebulun, Benjamin, Ephraim, and Manasseh.*

26. Which of Jacob's sons received a double blessing?
◇ *Joseph did because his two sons, Manasseh and Ephraim, both received a portion of land in Canaan.*

27. Which of Jacob's sons did not receive a portion of the promised land?
◇ *The tribe of Levi.*

28. What did the tribe of Levi receive instead of land?
◇ *God is Levi's inheritance.*

29. Did Jacob's firstborn son receive the blessing?
◇ *No, Joseph's son Ephraim received the physical blessing, and Judah received the promise that his descendant would rule.*

30. How many years were God's people enslaved in Egypt?
◇ *430 years.*

31. Who did God raise up to deliver the Jewish people?
◇ *Moses, from the tribe of Levi.*

❝ **32. Where did Moses grow up?**
  ◇ *Moses was adopted by Pharaoh's daughter and grew up in Egypt.*

❝ **33. How many plagues did God send to Egypt before the Jewish people were set free?**
  ◇ *10.*

❝ **34. What was the final plague?**
  ◇ *The death of the firstborn.*

❝ **35. Why did the Jewish children not die?**
  ◇ *They obeyed God, sacrificed a lamb, and placed the blood over their doors.*

❝ **36. Did the Jewish people leave Egypt in poverty?**
  ◇ *No, God had the Egyptians give them great wealth.*

❝ **37. What did the Jewish people do with that wealth?**
  ◇ *They joyfully gave it to build God's temple.*

❝ **38. What did God give to Moses on Mt. Sinai?**
  ◇ *The Torah (Law).*

❝ **39. Did Israel agree to keep the Torah?**
  ◇ *Yes.*

❝ **40. What did God promise to do if Israel did not keep their promise?**
  ◇ *To curse them and remove them from the land He promised Abraham.*

❝ **41. Did Israel keep the promise to obey the Torah (Law)?**
  ◇ *No, so they were sent into exile as God promised.*

❝ **42. Did God only promise exile if they disobeyed him?**
  ◇ *No, he also promised to bring the nation of Israel back to their land.*

43. Did God choose Israel because they were the best nation?
 No, God chose them because it gave Him pleasure.

44. How many feasts did God give Israel?
 Seven feasts or appointed times.

45. Are Gentiles required to keep the feasts?
 No, they were only for the tribes of Israel.

46. What are the spring feasts?
 Passover, Feast of Unleavened Bread, Firstfruits, and Feast of Weeks (also called Pentecost).

47. What are the fall feasts?
 Feast of Trumpets, Day of Atonement, and Feast of Tabernacles (also called Booths).

48. What do we learn from the Passover feast?
 Death passed over the firstborn of Jewish families, so God can deliver from death. And the Passover lamb pointed to Jesus.

49. What can we learn from the Feast of Unleavened Bread?
 Sin is the problem, and it needs to be removed. Jesus is the bread of life without sin. In Christ, believers are cleansed from sin.

50. What can we learn from the Feast of Firstfruits?
 God is the one who gives the harvest, and Jesus is the firstfruit of those who will rise from the dead.

51. What can we learn from the Feast of Weeks (Pentecost)?
 Fifty days after the Feast of Firstfruits, God gave the Torah, and 50 days after Jesus rose from the dead, God gave the Holy Spirit.

52. What is special about the fall feasts?
 Each teaches a past lesson and a future lesson.

❝ 53. What can we learn from the Feast of Trumpets?
◇ Israel celebrates the New Year, the birth of creation. One day, the trumpet will sound, and Jesus will come for his church.

❝ 54. What can we learn from the Day of Atonement?
◇ It was the one day a year when the high priest entered the Holy of Holies to make atonement for Israel, and it is the future day when Christ will physically return to earth.

❝ 55. What can we learn from the Feast of Tabernacles (Booths)?
◇ God provided in the wilderness when Israel left Egypt. One day, believers will dwell with God.

❝ 56. What is Jubilee?
◇ Every 50 years, liberty was proclaimed throughout all the land. All the property held by unpaid debts was returned, and all captives were released.

❝ 57. What did Moses do when Israel reached the border of the promised land?
◇ He sent 12 spies to spy out the land God was giving them.

❝ 58. What report did the 12 spies give who were sent out by Moses to inspect the promised land?
◇ Ten spies reported in fear, and two reported with faith in God.

❝ 59. What are the names of the two spies who reported in faith?
◇ Joshua, son of Nun, and Caleb from the tribe of Judah.

❝ 60. What did God do when the people listened to the 10 fearful spies?
◇ God made Israel wander in the wilderness for 40 years.

❝ 61. Did Moses lead Israel into the promised land?
◇ No, he disobeyed God and did not get to enter the promised land.

Family Discipleship Bible Stories

62. Who led Israel into the promised land?
- Joshua, son of Nun, led Israel into the promised land.

63. Did Israel drive out all the people dwelling in the promised land?
- No, after Joshua died, the next generation did not follow God and lost their battles.

64. What person did God send to help guide Israel after Joshua died?
- God sent judges who temporarily guided and delivered Israel from its enemies.

65. Name some judges from the Bible.
- Gideon, Deborah, Samson, and Samuel were all judges.

66. Who was Samuel?
- Samuel was the last judge and the prophet who anointed Israel's first king.

67. How did Israel reject God as their ruler?
- Israel asked for a king like the other nations.

68. Who was Israel's first king?
- God gave Saul from the tribe of Benjamin as Israel's first king.

69. Who was Israel's second king?
- David from the tribe of Judah.

70. What did God promise King David?
- God promised David that someone from his family line would be the Messiah, and His kingdom would endure forever.

71. Which of David's sons was his successor as king?
- Solomon, son of Bathsheba whose husband, Uriah, David had killed.

72. Who built the temple in Jerusalem?
- God let Solomon build it since David was a man of blood.

Jewish Bible Timeline (Ages 2+)

❝ **73. Did Solomon remain faithful?**
⬦ *No, Solomon did not heed God's instruction and was led into idolatry by foreign women.*

❝ **74. What consequence came as a result of Solomon's idolatry?**
⬦ *The kingdom was divided into two: the Northern Kingdom and the Southern Kingdom.*

❝ **75. How many tribes were in the Northern Kingdom?**
⬦ *10 tribes.*

❝ **76. What two tribes stayed faithful to David's line of rule?**
⬦ *The tribe of Benjamin and Judah.*

❝ **77. What was the capital city of the Northern Kingdom?**
⬦ *Samaria.*

❝ **78. What was the capital city of the Southern Kingdom?**
⬦ *Jerusalem was, is, and will always be the Holy City.*

❝ **79. Why were both kingdoms conquered?**
⬦ *Because of their continued idolatry, God scattered them as He promised He would.*

❝ **80. What year was the Northern Kingdom conquered by the Assyrians?**
⬦ *722 B.C.*

❝ **81. What year was the Southern Kingdom conquered by the Babylonians?**
⬦ *It was conquered in 607, and the temple was destroyed in 586 B.C.*

❝ **82. What other names does the Bible call the Northern Kingdom?**
⬦ *Ephraim and the House of Israel.*

❝ **83. What other name does the Bible call the Southern Kingdom?**
⬦ *Judah.*

❝ **84. How many kings ruled the Northern Kingdom?**
✧ God anointed 19 kings, but they were all evil, and none of them were from David's line.

❝ **85. How many kings ruled the Southern Kingdom?**
✧ God anointed 20 kings; six were good, and all were from David's line.

❝ **86. Did the tribes of Israel ever return to the land God promised them?**
✧ As God prophesied, Cyrus, king of Persia, let the Southern Kingdom exiles return to Israel. Many of the tribes of the Northern Kingdom returned, but not in the same prophetic manner.

❝ **87. Who was Elijah?**
✧ A prophet during wicked King Ahab's reign who performed many miracles and destroyed the prophets of Baal.

❝ **88. What did Ezekiel the prophet prophesy about?**
✧ Ezekiel warned of Israel's destruction but promised a new spirit would be given and that God would reunify Israel.

❝ **89. What did Isaiah prophesy?**
✧ Isaiah warned of Judah's destruction but gave many prophesies about the coming Messiah.

❝ **90. Who is Ezra?**
✧ A priestly descendant of Aaron who returned after the Babylonian exile and reintroduced the Torah (law) to Israel.

❝ **91. Who led the first return of the Jews from exile?**
✧ Zerubbabel led the first group of Jews back to Jerusalem after 70 years of exile and rebuilt the temple.

92. Who led the second return of the Jews from exile?
 ◇ Ezra the scribe led the second group of Jews back to Jerusalem and restored temple worship.

93. Who led the third return of the Jews from exile?
 ◇ Nehemiah led the third group of Jewish people back and rebuilt the temple wall.

94. Led by Nehemiah, how long did it take to rebuild the wall in Jerusalem?
 ◇ It only took 52 days.

95. Why was the second temple not as good as the first?
 ◇ It was without the ark of the covenant, so God's presence was not there like before.

96. Who is Esther?
 ◇ A young Jewish girl who become queen of Persia during the exile.

97. What did Esther do?
 ◇ Queen Esther listened to wise counsel, risked her life, and stopped a plan to exterminate all Jews.

98. Who was Malachi?
 ◇ Malachi was the final prophet God sent to Israel before sending John the Baptist 400 years later.

99. Who was John the Baptist?
 ◇ John the Baptist was the last Old Testament prophet and the forerunner of the Messiah.

100. What did John the Baptist say when Jesus approached him?
 ◇ "Behold, the Lamb of God, who takes away the sin of the world!" (John 1:29).

Family Discipleship Tools

Scripture Blessings

These blessings are simply scriptures that have been somewhat personalized so a father, mother, grandparents, or even older siblings can pray them over the children.

Genesis 48:15–16*

May the God before whom Abraham and Isaac walked,
    the God who has been my shepherd to this day,
    and who has delivered me from all harm
    bless you and make His name live on in you
    and in your children after you. Amen!

1 Kings 8:57–60*

May the Lord our God be with you as He has been with me.
May He never leave or forsake you.
May He incline your heart toward Him
    and cause you to walk in all His ways.
Day and night may your prayers be near Him.
May the Lord maintain your cause
    and the cause of all His people
So that you and all the peoples of the earth may know
    that the Lord is God, and there is none other! Amen!

Numbers 6:24–26*

The Lord will bless you and keep you.
The Lord will make His face shine on you
    and be gracious unto you.
The Lord will lift up His countenance upon you
    and give you peace. Amen!

Psalm 1*

May the Lord bless you!
May the Lord give you
    the courage not to walk in the counsel of the wicked;
    the faith not to stand in the path of sinners;
    and the resolve not to sit in the seat of mockers.
May you always delight in the law of the Lord
    and meditate on it day and night.
May you be like a tree planted by streams of water,
    which yields its fruit in season
    and whose leaf does not wither.
May the Lord prosper all that you do for His glory,
And may the Lord watch over your way
    all the days of your life
    so that you can stand in the day of judgment
    and join the assembly of the righteous forever. Amen!

Deuteronomy 28:3–6*

Blessed shall you be when you obey the Lord your God.
Blessed shall you be in the city.
Blessed shall you be in the country.

Blessed shall be your offspring.
Blessed shall be the work of your hands.
Blessed shall you be when you come in.
Blessed shall you be when you go out.
Blessed be the name of the Lord in your life, forever and ever. Amen!

Psalm 4*

May the Lord answer when you pray
    and relieve you in distress.
May He lift up the light of His countenance upon you
    and put gladness in your heart exceeding all earthly joy.
May the Lord establish you as a godly man/woman
    who trusts in Him.
May the Lord make you dwell in safety.
And when you lie down, may you sleep in peace. Amen!

Psalm 13:5–6*

May the Lord deal bountifully with you
    all the days of your life,
And may you always trust in the lovingkindness of the Lord.
In the days of sorrow and darkness,
    may you rejoice in the Lord's salvation
And sing to Him forever and ever. Amen!

Philippians 1:9–11

I bless you, that your love may abound more and more
    in real knowledge and all discernment,

so that you may approve the things that are excellent,
      in order to be sincere and blameless until the day of Christ;
May you be filled with the fruit of righteousness
   which comes through Jesus Christ, to the glory and praise of God.
Amen!

1 Thessalonians 3:10–13*

May God complete what is lacking in your faith
   so you will know God the Father, His Son Jesus
   so the Spirit of God will direct your way.
May the Lord cause you to increase and abound in love for all people,
   so that He may establish your heart without blame in holiness
   before God at the coming of the Lord Jesus. Amen!

Psalm 16*

May the Lord be your counselor all the days of your life.
Even in the night, may the Lord instruct your heart.
May you always set the Lord before you.
May the Lord always be at your right hand
   so that you will never be shaken.
May your heart be glad, your tongue rejoice,
   and your body rest secure.
May the Lord make known to you the path of life,
   fill you with joy in His presence,
   and give you pleasures at His right hand forever and ever. Amen!

Psalm 23*

May the LORD be your shepherd.
May He bless you with all that you need.
May He make you lie down in green pastures,
    lead you beside quiet waters, and restore your soul.
May He guide you in paths of righteousness
    for His name's sake.
May His rod and staff comfort you so that you fear no evil
    even when you walk
    through the valley of the shadow of death.
May the Lord prepare a table before you
    in the presence of your enemies.
May He anoint your head with oil.
May your cup of joy overflow continuously.
May the Lord's goodness and mercy follow you
    all the days of your life.
And may you dwell in the house of the Lord forever. Amen!

Psalm 103:1–5*

May you bless the Lord all the days of your life.
With all that is within you, may you bless His holy name.
May you never forget the benefits of Him who
    forgives your sins, heals your diseases, and
    redeems your life from destruction.
May the Lord satisfy your years with good things
    and crown your life with lovingkindness
    and tender mercies forever. Amen!

Psalm 112*

May you be a blessed man/woman who fears the Lord;
May you find great delight in the Lord's commands.
May your children be mighty in the land. Even to the next
　　generation, may you and your children be blessed.
May you find your wealth and your riches in God.
May you endure in righteousness forever.
Even in darkness may the light dawn for you.
May you be a gracious, compassionate
　　and righteous man/woman.
May you never be shaken. And may your name, [Insert Name],
　　be remembered by the Lord forever. Amen!

Psalm 121:5–8*

May the Lord watch over you.
May He be a shade at your right hand
　　so that the sun will not harm you by day
　　or the moon by night.
May the Lord keep you from all harm.
May He watch over your life.
May He watch over your coming and your going
　　both now and forever. Amen!

2 Thessalonians 1:11–12*

To this end I bless you in the name of the Lord:
That the Lord may make you worthy of His calling
　　fulfilling every good resolve and work of faith

by His power.
And may the name of the Lord Jesus be glorified in you
and you in Him, according to the grace
of our God and our Lord Jesus Christ,
to whom be glory forever and ever. Amen!

2 Thessalonians 2:16–17, 3:16*

May the Lord Jesus Christ Himself and God our Father,
who loves you and by His grace
gives you eternal encouragement and hope, comfort
and strengthen your heart in every good deed and word.
May the Lord of peace give you peace continually
and in every good circumstance.
And may the grace of the Lord Jesus Christ be with you
now and forever. Amen!

Hebrews 12:1*

May the Lord bless you like the mighty men and women of faith
who have gone before you.
May He give you:
grace to lay aside every encumbrance
and the sin which so easily entangles us;
endurance to run the race set before you;
and eyes fixed on Jesus,
who is the author and perfecter of faith! Amen!

Hebrews 13:20–21*

May the God of peace
   who brought up from the dead Jesus Christ our Lord
   through the blood of the eternal covenant
   equip you with every good thing to do His will,
   and work in you that which is pleasing in His sight
   through the power of Jesus Christ
   to whom be the glory forever and ever. Amen!

Psalm 125:1–2*

May the Lord increase your confidence in Him.
May you be like Mount Zion which cannot be shaken
   but endures forever.
As the mountains surround Jerusalem,
   may the Lord surround you
   both now and forever. Amen!

Psalm 15*

May you be blessed with the abiding presence of the Lord.
May your walk be blameless and your work be righteous.
May the Lord keep your tongue from sin
   and your relationships pure.
May you be honorable, loving, and generous with your money.
May the Lord keep you in His way
   so that you will not be shaken
   but endure in righteousness forever. Amen!

Romans 15:13*

May the God of hope fill you with all joy and peace
    as you trust in Him,
    so that you may abound in hope,
    through the power of the Holy Spirit. Amen!

2 Corinthians 13:14*

May the grace of the Lord Jesus Christ and the love of God
    and the fellowship of the Holy Spirit abide with you
    now and forever. Amen!

Ephesians 3:14–19*

And now, may our great and eternal Father bless you.
May He strengthen your inner being
    with power from the Holy Spirit.
May Christ dwell in your heart through faith.
May you be rooted and grounded in love
    so you will comprehend with all the saints
    the breadth and length and height and depth
    of the love of Christ, which surpasses knowledge.
May you be filled up to all the fullness of God
    according to the riches of His glory.
And may you exalt His glorious name forever and ever.
Amen!

Ephesians 3:20–21*

May God do for you exceeding abundantly
   beyond all that you ask or think,
   according to the power that works within you,
To Him be the glory
   in your life in Christ Jesus,
   and to all your lineage forever and ever. Amen!

Ephesians 6:10–17*

May you be a man/woman who is strong in the Lord
   and in His mighty power.
May you be blessed with the full armor of God
   so that you can resist the devil's schemes.
May you stand firm with the belt of truth
   buckled around your waist, and the breastplate
   of righteousness in place, and your feet
   fitted with the preparation of the gospel of peace.
May you take up the shield of faith, the helmet of salvation,
   and the sword of the Spirit, which is the word of God,
   so that when the day of evil comes,
   you will be able to stand your ground. Amen!

Ephesians 1:17–19

May the God of our Lord Jesus Christ, the Father of glory,
   give you the Spirit of wisdom and of revelation
   in the knowledge of Him.
And may the eyes of your heart be enlightened

so you will know what is the hope to which he has called you,
the riches of his glorious inheritance in the saints,
and the immeasurable greatness of his power. Amen!

1 Thessalonians 5:23–24*

May the God of peace sanctify you through and through.
May your whole spirit, soul, and body be preserved
   without blame at the coming of our Lord Jesus Christ.
And may you always trust the One who calls you
   and who has faithfully accomplished your redemption. Amen!

Psalm 51:1–2

May God have mercy on you according to his steadfast love,
   according to his abundant mercy.
And may he blot out your transgressions.
May our mighty God wash you thoroughly from
   your iniquity and cleanse you from all sin. Amen!

Psalm 51: 9–12

May God hide his face from your sin
   and blot out all of your iniquities.
May God create in you a clean heart,
   and renew your spirit from within.
May you never be cast away from God's presence.
May God give you the fullness of His Spirit,
   restore the joy of your salvation
   and uphold you with a willing spirit. Amen!

Deuteronomy 13:3–4

When the LORD God tests you to know
   whether you will follow Him with all your heart and soul,
May you walk after God, fear Him, keep His commandments,
   obey His voice.
May you serve Him and hold fast to Him all the days of your life. Amen!

Deuteronomy 31:6

May you be strong and courageous.
May you never fear or be in dread of any man
   because He goes with you
And may God never leave you or forsake you. Amen!

1 Timothy 4:12–13

May no one despise you because of your youth, but instead
   may you set the believers an example in speech,
   in conduct, in love, in faith, in purity.
May your life be marked with a devotion to the reading of scripture,
   exhorting and teaching others. Amen!

Ecclesiastes 3:1–8

I bless you with knowing that your Father's appointed time
   for everything in your life is beautiful.
I bless you with trusting His sovereign plan, even when you can't see it.
I bless you with joy in births, peace surrounding death,
   comfort during times of weeping, friends to laugh with,

wisdom to know when to gather, wisdom to know when to scatter, boldness to speak, strength to be silent, resolve to fight when needed, and may your heart rest during times of peace. Amen!

Psalm 91: 9–16

I bless you with the Lord as your dwelling place
    and in whom you find refuge.
May no evil befall you, may no sickness come near you.
May God's angels guard all your ways.
May you trample on all enemies that seem as strong as a lion
    or dangerous as a snake because God holds fast to you in love
    and will always deliver you.
I bless you with God's protection because He knows your name,
    answers when you call, gives you long life, satisfies you,
    and reveals to you His salvation. Amen!

John 17:14–17

Father, I have given these children your word,
    and if the world hates them it is because they are not of the world.
I do not ask that you take them out of the world,
    but that you keep them from the evil one.
Sanctify them in the truth; your word is truth. Amen!

1 Timothy 6:11–14

I bless you to pursue righteousness, godliness,
    faith, love, steadfastness, and gentleness.
I bless you to fight the good fight of the faith;

    to take hold of the eternal life that calls out to you
    and that you would make the good confession
    in the presence of many witnesses.
I bless you in the presence of God, who gives life to all things,
    and of Christ Jesus, to keep the commandments unstained
    and free from reproach until the appearing of our Lord Jesus Christ. Amen!

Proverbs 3:5–8

May you be blessed to trust in the Lord with all your heart,
    and not lean on your own understanding.
May you acknowledge him in all your ways.
May the Lord make your paths straight.
I bless you to not be wise in your own eyes
    but instead to fear the Lord and turn away from evil,
    bringing healing to your flesh and refreshment to your bones. Amen!

Proverbs 3:9–12

May you honor the LORD with your wealth
    and with the firstfruits of what you produce.
May the Lord then fill your barns with plenty
    so that your vats will be bursting with wine.
My son/daughter, may you never despise the Lord's discipline
    or be weary of His reproof, but see the Lord's reproof
as assurance of His love and delight in you. Amen!

Philippians 4:8–9

I bless you to think on these things; whatever is true,
    whatever is honorable, whatever is just, whatever is pure,
    whatever is lovely, whatever is commendable,
    if there is any excellence, if there is anything worthy of praise.
And may you practice these things as I try to live them before you
    so that the God of peace will be with you. Amen!

Ephesians 4:29–32

I bless your tongue that no corrupting talk will come out of your mouth,
    but only such as is good for building up, as fits the occasion,
    that it may give grace to those who hear.
And may you never grieve the Holy Spirit of God,
    by whom you were sealed for the day of redemption.
I bless you with a heart that puts away all bitterness and wrath
    and anger and clamor, slander, along with all malice,
That you would be kind to all, tenderhearted, forgiving others,
    as God in Christ forgives you. Amen!

Colossians 1:9–11

I bless you that you will be filled with the knowledge of God's will
    in all spiritual wisdom and understanding,
    so you will walk in a manner worthy of the Lord.
May you please God by bearing fruit in every good work
    and increase in the knowledge of God.
May God strengthen you with all power,
    according to his glorious might, for all endurance
    and patience with joy.

Colossians 1:12–13

I give thanks to the Father, who has qualified you
    to share in the inheritance of the saints in light.
I thank God that He will deliver you from
    the domain of darkness and transfer you to
    the kingdom of his beloved Son,
    in whom you may receive redemption,
    the forgiveness of sins. Amen!

1 Thessalonians 3:11–13

May our God and Father himself
    and our Lord Jesus direct your way.
And may the Lord make you increase
    and abound in love for all,
    so that he may establish your heart
    blameless in holiness. Amen!

Exodus 33:13

I bless you with favor in God's sight
    so he will show you His ways,
That you may know Him. Amen!

Psalm 91:14–16

I bless you with the ability to hold fast to God in love
    so He will deliver you.
May God protect you, because He knows your name.

When you call to Him, He will answer
    and when you are in trouble, He will be with you and rescue you.
May God bless you with long life,
    satisfy you, and show you His salvation. Amen!

Jonah 2:2

I bless you so that when you call out in your distress,
God will answer you.
And when you cry out to him,
He will hear your voice. Amen!

Joshua 1:5–6

I bless you that no man shall be able to stand before you
    all the days of your life.
May God be with you as He was with Moses,
    and may he never leave you or forsake you.
I bless you to be strong and courageous,
    to inherit all God has for you. Amen!

Joshua 1:7–8

May you be strong and very courageous, being careful
    to do according to all God asks of you
    and not to turn from it to the right hand or to the left,
    that you may have good success wherever you go.
May His word never depart from your mouth,
    but you shall meditate on it day and night,
    so that you will be careful to do all that is written.

For then He will make your way prosperous,
and then you will have good success. Amen!

Genesis 48:20 (for boys)

May God make you like Ephraim and Manasseh. Amen!

Proverbs 31:25–26, 29 (for girls)

May strength and dignity be your clothing as you laugh
   at the days to come.
May you open your mouth with wisdom as the teaching of
   kindness is on your tongue.
As girls all around you do well, I bless you to surpass them all.
Amen!

* These blessings are copied or adapted from *A Father's Guide to Blessing His Children* by David Michael.

Copyright © 1999, 2009 by Children Desiring God
1.877.400.1414
info@childrendesiringGod.org
www.childrendesiringGod.org

Scripture taken from the NEW AMERICAN STANDARD BIBLE®,
Copyright © The Lockman Foundation 1960, 1962, 1963, 1968, 1971, 1972, 1973, 1975, 1977, 1995; Used by permission.

Family Dictionary

Adoption – when God chooses to bring those who love and trust Jesus into His family and gives them His Spirit

Altar – a platform used to offer a sacrifice

Angel – a spirit created to serve God's purposes

Authority – the right to be in charge

Baptize – to immerse (cover) in water (a way of identifying with Jesus's death, burial, and resurrection)

Compassion – to see, care, and act when others are in need

Confess – to tell the truth about your sin without being asked

Confidence – sure and firm hope; believing and relying on God

Delight – when hearts are happy because God is in the highest place

Demon – an angel who chose to follow Satan instead of serving God

Devil – another name for Satan

Disciple – a person who does the things his teacher teaches no matter the cost

Discipline – God lovingly training His children to be more like Jesus

Eternity – without beginning or end

Exile – to be sent away from a certain place

Family Dictionary

Faith – Complete trust in what God says because of who He is

Fast – to not eat food or to eat only certain foods for a limited time

Generous – to joyfully and abundantly give to others

Glorify – to show, honor, and enjoy God as the greatest

God's children – those who love and trust Jesus

Grace – when God gives and does good to His children instead of giving what they deserve

Gratitude – being thankful to God no matter what He gives

Heart – where belief lives

Heaven – the place where God lives

Hebrew – a name for someone from the nation of Israel

Hell – a place of eternal fire and separation from God, created for demons

Holy – to be set apart (God is holy, or perfect and separate from sin)

Humility – happy when in the lowest place of importance

Jewish – referring to someone from the nation of Israel

Joy – delight that comes from knowing God no matter what situation one is in

Justice – fairness in giving a reward, discipline, or punishment

Obedience – doing what you're told right away with a great attitude

Patience – waiting without complaining, even when things get hard

Praise – to tell God how good He is

Prayer – conversation with God. We pray to the Father because of Jesus with the help of the Spirit

Pride – showing honor to yourself and enjoying yourself as the greatest

Reconcile – to make peace and remove separation between God and people

Redemption – to be bought back from slavery

Repentance – turning away from your own ways and following God's ways

Righteous – having a clean heart in all you do

Righteousness – to be free from guilt or sin

Sacrifice – a flawless animal, killed upon an altar in order to worship God

Satan – the lead angel who rebelled against God, who now deceives and accuses God's children

Sin – anything that comes from the heart that does not bring glory to God

Sovereign – having the right, power, and authority to be in charge

Soul – the part of a person that lives forever

Temptation – when sin seems good even though it is bad

Thanksgiving – to thank God for what He has done

Trust – to show faith by acting on what you believe

Wisdom – to know what God thinks about something and how to act upon it

Songs for the Family
(Look any of these up on YouTube. Suggested performer is in parentheses)

"Here Is Love" by William Rees (Bethel Church)
"Amazing Grace" by John Newton (Wintley Phipps)
"The Solid Rock" by Edward Mote (Austin Stone)
"I Stand Amazed" by Charles Gabriel (Chris Tomlin)
"Jesus Paid It All" by Elvina Hall (David Crowder)
"In Christ Alone" by Townend and Getty (Lauren Daigle)
"10,000 Reasons" by Matt Redman and Jonas Myrin
"How Deep the Father's Love for Us" by Stuart Townend (Fernando Ortega)
"Go Tell It on the Mountain" by John W. Work Jr. (MercyMe)
"Doxology" by Thomas Ken (David Crowder Band)
"Joyful, Joyful, We Adore Thee" by Henry Van Dyke (Casting Crowns)
"How Great Thou Art" by Stuart Hine (Carrie Underwood)

Summary of Old Testament Books

Pentateuch – First five books

- **Genesis** – creation, the fall, the flood, spread of the nations, the beginning of the Hebrew nation, and enslavement of God's people

- **Exodus** – God delivers Israel from bondage; Israel's birth as a nation, God's covenant with Israel, giving of the Torah, and instructions to build the tabernacle

- **Leviticus** – instructions on the sacrificial system and the priesthood, and instructions on moral purity

- **Numbers** – the journey to the promised land; at Mt. Sinai, Israel makes the golden calf; God disciplines the nation with 40 years of wandering in the desert

- **Deuteronomy** – God's commentary on the covenant

Historical Books – 12 books

- **Joshua** – the conquest and the allotting of the promised land of Canaan

- **Judges** – the first 300 years in the promised land and the time of the judges; Israel fails to drive out the people of Canaan, and everyone does what is right in their own eyes

- **Ruth** – the story of the Messianic family of David; Boaz, a kinsman redeemer, redeems a Moabite named Ruth

Summary of Old Testament Books

The next six books trace the time from Samuel to the captivity

- **1 Samuel** – Israel transitions from judges to having a king; the prophet Samuel anoints Saul as king, Saul disobeys, God rejects Saul, and Samuel anoints David
- **2 Samuel** – David's reign as king; David commits adultery and murder; the rise of his son Solomon
- **1 Kings** – Division of the kingdom; Solomon and the nation Israel become powerful and famous; Solomon's idolatry leads to a divided kingdom (10 tribes to the north and two to the south)
- **2 Kings** – History of the divided kingdom; All 19 kings of Israel were bad; in Judah, eight of 20 rulers were good, and the rest were idolatrous; God exiles both kingdoms from the land; Assyrians conquer the North, and Babylon conquers the South.
- **1 Chronicles** – focuses on the genealogies of the Southern Kingdom and recounts much of the books of Samuel and Kings
- **2 Chronicles** – History of the Southern Kingdom of Judah; recounts the life of Solomon, the building of the temple, and of Judah's history

The next three books deal with Israel's restoration.

- **Ezra** – records the Jews' return from the Babylonian exile in two separate groups and the rebuilding of the temple; Zerubbabel led the first group, and Ezra led the second group
- **Nehemiah** – continued story of return of the Jews to Jerusalem; Nehemiah rebuilds the wall of Jerusalem; Ezra reads the Torah (law), and there is a great revival
- **Esther** – while in exile God delivers His people; Queen Esther, a Hebrew married to a Persian king, listens to wise counsel and risks her life, resulting in the Jews escaping extinction

Poetical – five books

- **Job** – God in His sovereignty tests a righteous man by allowing him to be directly attacked by Satan; God's mercy is found in Job's deepened relationship with God
- **Psalms** – written mostly by King David, a collection of prayers, songs, and meditations
- **Proverbs** – written mostly by King Solomon, a collection of poems and wise sayings useful in everyday life
- **Ecclesiastes** – summary of King Solomon's search for the meaning of life; he concludes that all is vanity and counsels all to enjoy God's gifts and fear and obey Him
- **Song of Solomon** – poetic song between Solomon and his bride shadowing the love between God and His people

Prophetic – 17 books (major prophets and minor prophets)

Major Prophets – five books

- **Isaiah** – (to Southern Kingdom) proclaims God's coming judgment on the Southern Kingdom by Babylon and gives prophetic insight to the coming Messiah
- **Jeremiah** – (to Southern Kingdom) final plea for Judah's repentance before eventual judgment; prophesies God's plan for a new covenant and the coming king
- **Lamentations** – five poems of painful lament over the desolation of Jerusalem; describes the defeat and fall of Jerusalem

- **Ezekiel** – during Babylonian exile, Ezekiel pronounces judgment on Israel and surrounding nations; Ezekiel provides a vision of the future millennial kingdom and tells of a restoration of a remnant of Israel
- **Daniel** – historic account of how God protected Israel during exile; many visions show God's sovereign power over all the kingdoms of the earth

Minor Prophets – 12 books

- **Hosea** – (Northern Kingdom) Hosea's marriage to an unfaithful wife is a shadow of Israel's unfaithfulness to God and His unfailing love
- **Joel** – (pre-exile Southern Kingdom) a terrifying account of future judgment if Judah does not repent; gives hope of the coming kingdom
- **Amos** – (Northern Kingdom) warned Israel of its coming judgment due to their oppression of the poor and their lack of justice
- **Obadiah** – (Edom) proclaims destruction for Edom, a neighboring Gentile nation, for taking pleasure in God's judgment of Jerusalem
- **Jonah** – (Nineveh) proclaims a coming judgment on Nineveh if they do not repent; Nineveh listens and is spared, to the displeasure of Jonah
- **Micah** – (Northern and Southern Kingdoms) proclaims destruction for Israel and Judah for their idolatry and lack of justice; promises restoration and prophesies that Messiah will be born in Bethlehem
- **Nahum** – (Nineveh) prophesies destruction to Nineveh; Nineveh repented after Jonah's preaching, but their return to wickedness brought the judgment of God
- **Habakkuk** – (Southern Kingdom) questions God for not addressing Judah's wickedness; questions God's use of the Babylonians to judge Judah; with no answer, Habakkuk rests in God's salvation

- **Zephaniah** – (Southern Kingdom) announces the Day of the Lord against Judah and the nations; God will eventually bless the nations, and a remnant of Judah will be restored

- **Haggai** – after returning from exile, Haggai says God is withholding prosperity because they are building their own houses first; the people listen, and God responds with encouragement and blessing

- **Zechariah** – encourages the Jews to complete the temple; contains many messianic prophecies; speaks of Gentiles worshiping God

- **Malachi** – After returning from exile, Malachi delivers a final message of coming judgment to a disobedient people and tells of a forerunner to the Messiah

Scripture Memory Passages

John 1:1–14

[1] In the beginning was the Word, and the Word was with God, and the Word was God. [2] He was in the beginning with God. [3] All things were made through him, and without him was not any thing made that was made. [4] In him was life, and the life was the light of men. [5] The light shines in the darkness, and the darkness has not overcome it.

[6] There was a man sent from God, whose name was John. [7] He came as a witness, to bear witness about the light, that all might believe through him. [8] He was not the light, but came to bear witness about the light.

[9] The true light, which gives light to everyone, was coming into the world. [10] He was in the world, and the world was made through him, yet the world did not know him. [11] He came to his own, and his own people did not receive him. [12] But to all who did receive him, who believed in his name, he gave the right to become children of God, [13] who were born, not of blood nor of the will of the flesh nor of the will of man, but of God.

[14] And the Word became flesh and dwelt among us, and we have seen his glory, glory as of the only Son from the Father, full of grace and truth.

Psalm 23

¹ The Lord is my shepherd; I shall not want.
²   He makes me lie down in green pastures.
He leads me beside still waters.
³   He restores my soul.
He leads me in paths of righteousness
    for his name's sake.
⁴ Even though I walk through the valley of the shadow of death,
    I will fear no evil,
for you are with me;
    your rod and your staff,
    they comfort me.
⁵ You prepare a table before me
    in the presence of my enemies;
you anoint my head with oil;
    my cup overflows.
⁶ Surely goodness and mercy shall follow me
    all the days of my life,
and I shall dwell in the house of the Lord
    forever.

Psalm 150

¹ Praise the Lord!
Praise God in his sanctuary;
    praise him in his mighty heavens!
² Praise him for his mighty deeds;
    praise him according to his excellent greatness!
³ Praise him with trumpet sound;

praise him with lute and harp!
⁴ Praise him with tambourine and dance;
   praise him with strings and pipe!
⁵ Praise him with sounding cymbals;
   praise him with loud clashing cymbals!
⁶ Let everything that has breath praise the LORD!
Praise the LORD!

Proverbs 3:1–12

¹ My son, do not forget my teaching,
   but let your heart keep my commandments,
² for length of days and years of life
   and peace they will add to you.
³ Let not steadfast love and faithfulness forsake you;
   bind them around your neck;
   write them on the tablet of your heart.
⁴ So you will find favor and good success
   in the sight of God and man.
⁵ Trust in the LORD with all your heart,
   and do not lean on your own understanding.
⁶ In all your ways acknowledge him,
   and he will make straight your paths.
⁷ Be not wise in your own eyes;
   fear the LORD, and turn away from evil.
⁸ It will be healing to your flesh
   and refreshment to your bones.
⁹ Honor the LORD with your wealth
   and with the firstfruits of all your produce;
¹⁰ then your barns will be filled with plenty,

and your vats will be bursting with wine.
¹¹ My son, do not despise the LORD's discipline
   or be weary of his reproof,
¹² for the LORD reproves him whom he loves,
   as a father the son in whom he delights.

Psalm 27:1–6

¹ The LORD is my light and my salvation;
   whom shall I fear?
The LORD is the stronghold of my life;
   of whom shall I be afraid?
² When evildoers assail me
   to eat up my flesh,
my adversaries and foes,
   it is they who stumble and fall.
³ Though an army encamp against me,
   my heart shall not fear;
though war arise against me,
   yet I will be confident.
⁴ One thing have I asked of the LORD,
   that will I seek after:
that I may dwell in the house of the LORD
   all the days of my life,
to gaze upon the beauty of the LORD
   and to inquire in his temple.
⁵ For he will hide me in his shelter
   in the day of trouble;
he will conceal me under the cover of his tent;
   he will lift me high upon a rock.

⁶ And now my head shall be lifted up
    above my enemies all around me,
and I will offer in his tent
    sacrifices with shouts of joy;
I will sing and make melody to the Lord.

Colossians 1:15–20

¹⁵He is the image of the invisible God, the firstborn of all creation. ¹⁶ For by him all things were created, in heaven and on earth, visible and invisible, whether thrones or dominions or rulers or authorities—all things were created through him and for him. ¹⁷ And he is before all things, and in him all things hold together.¹⁸ And he is the head of the body, the church. He is the beginning, the firstborn from the dead, that in everything he might be preeminent. ¹⁹ For in him all the fullness of God was pleased to dwell, ²⁰ and through him to reconcile to himself all things, whether on earth or in heaven, making peace by the blood of his cross.

Romans 12:9–18

⁹ Let love be genuine. Abhor what is evil; hold fast to what is good. ¹⁰ Love one another with brotherly affection. Outdo one another in showing honor. ¹¹ Do not be slothful in zeal, be fervent in spirit, serve the Lord. ¹² Rejoice in hope, be patient in tribulation, be constant in prayer. ¹³ Contribute to the needs of the saints and seek to show hospitality.

¹⁴ Bless those who persecute you; bless and do not curse them. ¹⁵ Rejoice with those who rejoice, weep with those who weep. ¹⁶ Live in harmony with one another. Do not be haughty, but associate with the lowly. Never be

wise in your own sight. [17] Repay no one evil for evil, but give thought to do what is honorable in the sight of all. [18] If possible, so far as it depends on you, live peaceably with all.

Isaiah 53:1–6

[1] Who has believed what he has heard from us?
    And to whom has the arm of the Lord been revealed?
[2] For he grew up before him like a young plant,
    and like a root out of dry ground;
he had no form or majesty that we should look at him,
    and no beauty that we should desire him.
[3] He was despised and rejected by men,
    a man of sorrows and acquainted with grief;
and as one from whom men hide their faces
    he was despised, and we esteemed him not.
[4] Surely he has borne our griefs
    and carried our sorrows;
yet we esteemed him stricken,
    smitten by God, and afflicted.
[5] But he was pierced for our transgressions;
    he was crushed for our iniquities;
upon him was the chastisement that brought us peace,
    and with his wounds we are healed.
[6] All we like sheep have gone astray;
    we have turned—every one—to his own way;
and the Lord has laid on him
    the iniquity of us all.

Galatians 5:22–23

22 But the fruit of the Spirit is love, joy, peace, patience, kindness, goodness, faithfulness, 23 gentleness, self-control; against such things there is no law.

Romans 8:28–39

28 And we know that for those who love God all things work together for good, for those who are called according to his purpose. 29 For those whom he foreknew he also predestined to be conformed to the image of his Son, in order that he might be the firstborn among many brothers. 30 And those whom he predestined he also called, and those whom he called he also justified, and those whom he justified he also glorified.

31 What then shall we say to these things? If God is for us, who can be against us? 32 He who did not spare his own Son but gave him up for us all, how will he not also with him graciously give us all things? 33 Who shall bring any charge against God's elect? It is God who justifies. 34 Who is to condemn? Christ Jesus is the one who died—more than that, who was raised—who is at the right hand of God, who indeed is interceding for us. 35 Who shall separate us from the love of Christ? Shall tribulation, or distress, or persecution, or famine, or nakedness, or danger, or sword? 36 As it is written,

> "For your sake we are being killed all the day long;
> we are regarded as sheep to be slaughtered."

37 No, in all these things we are more than conquerors through him who loved us. 38 For I am sure that neither death nor life, nor angels nor rulers, nor things present nor things to come, nor powers, 39 nor height nor depth, nor anything else in all creation, will be able to separate us from the love of God in Christ Jesus our Lord.

In Conclusion

Final Message to Parents

In order to be a foster parent and remain licensed by the state, you must attend various types of training. They range from behavioral management to learning about psychotropic medications. During the course of our time as foster parents, my wife and I attended a nine-week training called Empowered to Connect. Although it was geared toward parents who have children "from hard places," we found it applicable to any parent. Before the first week of the class, we were asked to write down our goal in parenting. In the first class, one parent shared her well-meaning parental goal, that her child would be able to bounce back from adversity.

Being able to bounce back from adversity is a good thing, but the people in the group were believers who had adopted or were in the process of adopting. We wondered how there could be parenting goals in this class that were void of God and His desires for parents. But by God's grace, the class helped every parent, including us, to deepen their understanding of God's desires in parenting and how to get there. I believe we find the purest picture of what God desires in the story of Samson. In Judges 13, an angel comes to a woman who was barren and tells her that she will have a child that has a purpose from God. She tells her husband, and he does what we all would do—asks God to send the angel to him so he knows what to do:

> Then Manoah prayed to the Lord and said, "O Lord, please let the man of God whom you sent come again to us and teach us what we are to do with the child who will be born." And God listened to the voice of Manoah, and the angel of God came again to the woman as she sat in the field. But

Manoah her husband was not with her. So the woman ran quickly and told her husband, "Behold, the man who came to me the other day has appeared to me." And Manoah arose and went after his wife and came to the man and said to him, "Are you the man who spoke to this woman?" And he said, "I am." And Manoah said, "Now when your words come true, what is to be the child's manner of life, and what is his mission?" And the angel of the Lord said to Manoah, "Of all that I said to the woman let her be careful. She may not eat of anything that comes from the vine, neither let her drink wine or strong drink, or eat any unclean thing. All that I commanded her let her observe" (Judges 13:8–14).

What we find here is that the angel from God doesn't lay out a step-by-step plan from birth but rather the call to observe all he commanded her to observe. In essence, he tells the parents to be faithful to the Lord's commands. Too often as parents, we forget that our faithfulness to God is vital to our role as parents. If you remember the story, Samson's story wasn't really a picture of obedience. In fact, he is more a picture of pride gone awry leading to an early death. Do you think his parents failed as parents? To be honest, much like us, Samson made his own poor decisions despite what he was taught. The crazy thing is that the next time we hear of Samson is in Hebrews 11, the so-called hall of fame for the faithful. How can that be? Because in the end, he fulfilled the purposes of God. He judged Israel for 20 years and ended up humble before the Lord.

Do you think Samson's parents were ultimately proud that God considered Samson faithful despite his series of poor choices? I'm sure they were. You see, even a perfect father has children that make poor choices despite what they are taught and how it was taught (see Gen. 3). But parents need to keep in mind that God's purposes are sometimes unknown, so we can't let visible results drive the measurement of our successful parenting. What we have to do is focus on being faithful to God in every role we have—father, mother, husband, wife, vocation counselor, volunteer, servant. In other words, to be a good parent, we should strive to be better servants of Christ.

One of our problems is that many of us have hurts that have not been healed, and we are carrying those wounds into our parenting lens. We don't see God correctly and don't understand how He sees us, either. This poor theology of God and His redeemed enters our daily interaction with our kids, and we sometimes feel hopeless. The truth is that God knows our hearts, our children's hearts, and His purposes, so we must maintain hope that He has it all under control. According to Acts 17, He divinely chose to match us not only with our children but also with the parents who might have been an active part of our hurts as well.

So what do we do? Should we just count on God to work it all out? Not at all! Instead, we actively war against our flesh, seek out healing for our hurts, and strive to point our children to the perfect Father. We do this by being intentional in as many areas as we can. Being intentional is a lost art in parenting. It is easy to forget that children are learning all the time, not just during designed teaching times. But being intentional isn't just what we do. We must explain why we are doing the things we do. For instance, placing a child in time-out because he or she disobeyed could be seen as punishment to a child. It is completely different to speak to the child about your love that sent him or her to the time-out. Children must know that God doesn't punish His children but gives discipline to train His children. The time-out was not meant to punish but to discipline. Their actions reveal they believe the lie that their way is better than God's (Rom. 1). You desire to be with them, but sin separates us from God, and the time-out was a picture of that separation. God sent His Son to end that separation for those who repent and believe. If children repent of their disobedience, their time-out ends, and we ask God for forgiveness together.

This type of intentionality can be tiresome, but after all, doesn't faithfulness require us to speak of God's ways from morning until night (Deut. 6:4–7)? Sure, we wish there was a step-by-step guide for every situation we face, but in end, all of us come to a place where we are clueless about how to be faithful in a particular situation. We must always remember that being faithful is not measured in an instant but over time. We are being transformed into the image of His Son more and more. The more we are like Jesus, the more we image the Father. The more we image the Father, the more faithful we are as parents. Oh, to be like Him!

God is slow to anger and abounding in steadfast love. Our heavenly Father never disciplines us with a scowl on His face, and neither should we scowl at our children. Yes, we should catechize our children and do daily devotionals, but it will be our daily parenting that will teach what we actually believe about God more than anything. Let us desire to be faithful, leave the results to Him, and trust that even our best parenting moments won't be enough to save their souls. Their salvation is not by our works but by His grace alone.

May grace abound in our homes!

Additional Resources for Your Home

There are many great resources we could recommend, but these should give you a good starting point.

For Parents

Family Shepherds: Calling and Equipping Men to Lead Their Homes — Voddie Baucham Jr.
Directed solely to a father, this book is explained well in the title.

Family Driven Faith: Doing What It Takes to Raise Sons and Daughters Who Walk with God — Voddie Baucham Jr.
A challenging read that calls parents to get into the game and raise their children as God calls them. Toward the end, the book does push some family and church integration. The vast majority of the book is very insightful.

Shepherding a Child's Heart — Tedd Tripp
This book comes back to the gospel and the true nature of our children's hearts and how God graciously provides a solution in the scriptures.

This Momentary Marriage: A Parable of Permanence — John Piper
This is a fabulous book that properly roots marriage within the context of God's plans and purposes. It is a must-read for any parent wanting to display the gospel daily to their children.

Treasuring God in Our Traditions — Noël Piper
Gives parents a needed reminder that what we pass along to our children is very important.

The Connected Child: Bring Hope and Healing to Your Adoptive Family — Karyn B. Purvis, Ph.D. David R. Cross, Ph.D., and Wendy Lyons Sunshine
Written for adoptive parents, this book is a must-read for any parent looking to parent with the goal of reaching a child's heart.

For the Family

Bibles

The Jesus Story Book Bible: Every Story Whispers His Name — Sally Lloyd-Jones
This book works its way through the Bible showing how everything points to Jesus. Great for pre-school age and early elementary.

The Gospel Story Bible: Discovering Jesus in the Old and New Testaments — Marty Machowski
A wide range of stories from both the Old and New Testaments. Provides questions after each story to foster teaching. Good for school age kids, especially those who read on their own.

Long Story Short: Ten-Minute Devotions to Draw Your Family to God — Marty Machowski
Easy 10-minute devotionals that any parent can do.

Books

The Big Book of Questions & Answers about Jesus — Ferguson Sinclair
A great resource for any family when it comes to answering questions and doing devotionals.

Big Truths for Young Hearts: Teaching and Learning the Greatness of God — Bruce A. Ware
Systematically gives parents chapters to read and helps them teach theology to their children.

Halfway Herbert – Francis Chan
A great little kid's book that introduces kids to the fact that they need Jesus and the Spirit to give them a whole heart.

The Big Red Tractor and the Little Village – Francis Chan
This kid's book masterfully teaches kids the power of the Holy Spirit available to us.

Ronnie Wilson's Gift – Francis Chan
A touching kid's story that shows what it looks like to serve Christ while here on earth.

Jesus is Coming Back! – Debby Anderson
A fun book for toddlers that teaches them that Jesus will return.

Little Pilgrim's Progress: From John Bunyan's Classic – Helen L. Taylor
An absolutely great read for young readers but even better if read by a parent. Read a chapter or two a night after dinner or use it as a devotional by asking questions after each chapter.

God Knows My Name – Debby Anderson
Another fun book for toddlers that teaches them about God.

A Forever Home for Antonio: A Gospel Adoption Journey – Chris Chavez
A gospel-centered kids book on adoption. A great story to help parents build a framework to explain adoption.

The Gospel Advent Book – Chris Chavez
A 25-day family devotional written to help parents teach about the coming of the Messiah.

Golly's Folly: The Prince Who Wanted It All – Eleazar Ruiz and Rebekah Ruiz
www.gollysfolly.com

Incredibly illustrated book based on the book of Ecclesiastes. There is also a workbook available.

Music

Seeds Family Worship
- www.seedsfamilyworship.com
- Fun, scripture-based songs on CD that can help your family sing and worship together
- Can be found on iTunes as well

Jesus Came to Save Sinners
- Download for free at www.thevillagechurch.net/resources/music/
- Fun and teaches theology of the gospel and God's character
- Can be found on iTunes as well

Bethel Music Kids
- www.bethelmusic.com/albums/come-alive/
- Fun and engaging kid versions of their music
- Can be found on iTunes as well

Crazy Praise CDs
- Can be found on iTunes

Acknowledgments

Luke Damoff — Your theological pushback and encouragement helped me produce a much more loving resource for parents. Your thoughts challenged me and actually helped me understand my own marriage in a deeper way. We didn't have to agree on everything, but we did have to be honest in our thoughts, and you did that with grace. Thank you for your obedience to what the Bible says and not what I wanted it to say.

John Blase — I am immensely blessed to have the Lord deliver an editor of your caliber to my doorstep. You were able to help me convey thoughts with much needed clarity. Any reader who finds any flaws with the writing must understand that you were working with an untrained writer, and you are to be commended for your work. You are a blessing, and I am thankful you accepted this project.

Mike Brown — Who would have guessed that two fraternity knuckleheads would one day collaborate on a Bible-teaching resource for parents? Your gifting has always been evident, and I pray that many children are inspired by your wonderful artwork. I am so glad to have taken on this project with a friend and brother in the Lord.

Antonio Chavez Jr. — Dad, I'll never know how life would have been if you had not been killed in an accident when I was 6. Who you were when you were alive remains a mystery to me in so many ways. By all accounts, you were the man I hope to be one day. But know this, your absence has been a driver in my family.

Acknowledgments

It wasn't until age 39 that I grieved your being gone, wondering if we would have been friends if we met that day. That weekend filled with tears is a marker in my life, and as much as I wish you had been there when I was growing up, I can now thank God for your early death. I now have a heart to be a father that I might not have had, and this book is rooted in that heart. Whatever DNA I have that reflects God's goodness, I thank you for it and hope to be your friend when Jesus returns.

Our Kickstarter Contributors – A special thank you to all listed here and the many others who gave to help bring this project to life.

Joe and Lindsay Rodden
The Clarke Family
The Shanks Family
The Rozelle Family
Jinohn Renea
Ben and Gina Killmer
The Embry Family
The Berend Family
The Barba Family
The Rabalais Family
The Bowman Family
The Hull Family

The Ullmann Family
The Pierce Family
The White Family
The Ayers Family
The Miller Family
Rich and Staci Cass
The Michaelis Family
The Schroyer Family
The Lee Family
Cass Family Charitable Trust
The Juergens Family
The Jung Family

About the Illustrator

Michael Brown is an award-winning actor/director of theatre and film, as well as an author/illustrator. Michael has had a cartoon syndicated by King Features and a feature film distributed by Lionsgate. He enjoys the unique challenges each artistic medium brings. Michael lives in Texas with his beautiful wife, Cheree, and his children: Abby, Luke, Lydia, and Phoebe. He never has to look far from the cast of characters living in his house to find fresh artistic inspiration. Visit Michael online at www.browncowproductions.com.

www.ingramcontent.com/pod-product-compliance
Lightning Source LLC
Chambersburg PA
CBHW041410300426
44114CB00028B/2973